THE
PURPOSE
CODE

THE
PURPOSE
CODE

HOW TO UNLOCK MEANING, MAXIMIZE HAPPINESS, AND LEAVE A LASTING LEGACY

JORDAN GRUMET, MD

HARRIMAN HOUSE LTD
3 Viceroy Court
Bedford Road
Petersfield
Hampshire
GU32 3LJ
GREAT BRITAIN
Tel: +44 (0)1730 233870

Email: enquiries@harriman-house.com
Website: harriman.house

First published in 2025.
Copyright © Jordan Grumet

Hardback ISBN: 978-1-80409-085-5
Paperback ISBN: 978-1-80409-086-2
eBook ISBN: 978-1-80409-087-9

British Library Cataloguing in Publication Data
A CIP catalogue record for this book can be obtained from the British Library.

Illustrations by Janis Ozolins

Important Note to the Reader

This publication is sold with the understanding that neither the author nor the publisher is providing specific psychiatric, legal, financial, medical, or other professional services to the reader. The information in this book is not meant to replace the advice of certified or licensed professionals with the requisite expertise. We encourage you to seek such an advisor as related to both mental, physical, and financial health as needed.

While many of the stories in this book are based on real experiences, the names, medical diagnoses, and financial situations described have been changed to respect privacy. Furthermore, some facts in the stories have been altered to maintain narrative cohesion without materially affecting the reality and difficulty of the situations or the importance of the messages.

CONTENTS

INTRODUCTION:
THE TRIUMPH OF THE
LITTLE BECKONINGS

Sometimes dinner can change the course of your life. On November 3, 1948, Julia Child sat down next to her husband, Paul, to eat her first meal on French soil. Her life was about to take a remarkable turn.

At that point, she could be described as a woefully unskilled cook at best. Her main experience in the kitchen consisted of helping to create the formula for shark repellant during a short-lived career as a spy in what would eventually become the Central Intelligence Agency. She was not a failure in life (though her attempts to become a novelist had not gone well). But she was lost.

That fateful meal at *La Couronne* (The Crown) in the medieval city of Rouen, northern France, changed everything. Julia called it "the most exciting meal of my life"[1]—and not because it was delicious (though it was). It was the moment she developed an inkling of her deepest sense of purpose.

"It came upon me that that was what I was looking for all my life. One taste of that food and I never turned back."

Like a flash of lightning, Julia had the sudden realization that she wanted to cook; and not just any dishes, but the dishes of the most storied cuisine in the world—France.[2] She was not spurred by grand plans of amassing wealth or changing the world (though, as it turned out, that all happened nonetheless). Her ambitions were more modest, and yet more powerful: to cook delicious food.

Success was slow and difficult. Julia failed her first exam at Le Cordon Bleu. It took her over ten years to write her classic book, *Mastering the Art of French Cooking*.

The idea of quitting, however, never occurred to Julia. She was having too much fun on her gastronomic adventures. Her true measure of success wasn't the books and television shows, or all the money she eventually made from them. It was the joy of cooking and the people she touched along the way.

"I don't think about whether people will remember me or not. I've been an okay person. I've learned a lot. I've taught people a thing or two. That's what's important. Sooner or later the public will forget you, the memory of you will fade. What's important is the individuals you've influenced along the way."

———————

Julia Child's sense of purpose is a stunning example of something I believe we can all experience. But discussing purpose with audiences large and small doesn't always lead to a positive response. In fact, the most common response is wildly negative.

I clearly remember the first time I experienced this reaction. I had just stepped off stage at a weekend seminar in Julien, California, having given a 45-minute talk about building financial independence and living a regret-free life, when an audience member sidled up to me as I walked toward the back of the auditorium.

Her upper lip was curled into a snarl. Somehow, my talk had gotten her into such a lather that she wasn't going to pass up the opportunity to confront me in person. I was shocked: the purpose of the talk was to help people. Shrinking back, I braced myself. As she opened her mouth to speak, I had no idea what she was going to say.

"I'm so sick of people telling me to find my purpose. I don't know my purpose and it's stressing me out!"

No one had ever said that to me before. But over the next year—as I went from conference to conference, podcast to podcast, and speaking engagement to speaking engagement, sharing how the ideas in my first book could help people—I kept hearing it.

It became overwhelmingly clear that most people struggle to find their sense of purpose, and struggle even harder to integrate this vision into anything they would call *happiness*. Curious, I dug into the data. It turns out that even though having a sense of purpose can increase lifespan, health, and happiness, it is also associated with anxiety in over 91% of people at some point in their lives. I was dumbfounded. How can we explain this paradox?

I began to realize that even those who have been able to see past the mirage of wealth and start searching for what really is important in life find themselves facing a larger and even more frightening obstacle. They know that happiness and purpose are intimately tied together but they can't quite explain how. They understand the term *purpose*, but have no idea how to take action to discover what it means in their lives.

For most people, purpose has become a kind of indecipherable code, sealing away true fulfillment and lasting happiness. But the purpose code is one that can be cracked. And anyone can do it. This book will show you how.

Why am I so sure? Well, as this book will share with you, there are many incredible (but unheard) true stories, numerous fascinating (but often overlooked) studies, the perspectives of many wise (but sometimes neglected) writers, and much more besides that all attest to this and will help you crack the code … But first, it's because I know from my own experience.

Let me tell you a story about a man called Roman and the lives he changed.

THE MAN WHO CHANGED THE WORLD WITH BASEBALL CARDS

Back in middle school, an awkward kid on the cusp of teenagerdom, I met a man who changed my life forever without intending to. He had stumbled upon his own sense of purpose and, because of it, was making his mark on the world—and those around him.

Roman was the picture of an aging athlete. His twenties had seen his muscles soften and the beginnings of a belly develop on his otherwise lean frame. His boyish face was patient and kind. He always seemed to be about to smile.

Roman would have described himself as a people person. In fact, it's probably why he went into the antiques business in the first place. His high-school tenure as a top football player ended with the unfortunate twist of an ankle. Yet his natural affability—combined with furniture-refinishing skills learned from his carpenter father—made owning an antiques store in the Chicago suburbs more or less viable.

He spent his days hanging out in the store, refinishing old furniture in the back when foot traffic was slow, and buying and selling various doodads when he saw the opportunity to make a buck. One day, while cleaning out an old dresser in preparation for sanding, he scouted out a long-forgotten box of baseball cards tucked away in the far recesses of the bottom drawer. A quick call to the seller confirmed that the cards were unwanted and Roman was free to do with them as he pleased. While he often caught the Cubbies on the radio or the small portable television at the checkout counter, he had no idea how to place a value on the forgotten box of cards.

A few days later, a surly teenager accompanying his mother into the store provided a tidy solution. He offered Roman $100 for the whole lot. Feeling that luck was upon him—which it truly was, though not for the reason he thought—he parted with the haphazard collection without hesitation.

Now, as any of you reading this who happen to have a surly teenager at home will have experienced, they aren't afraid to let you know when you have made a mistake. This young kid—Ryan was his name—was quick to spread a few cards on the counter right in front of Roman and explain why the collection was worth far more than $100.

And that's when it suddenly clicked. Roman knew that he was meant to buy and sell baseball cards. He couldn't explain why exactly. Maybe it was the memory of bending them into the spokes of his bike when he rode around the neighborhood with his friends in elementary school; or the touch of his father's hand as he was dragged through the bleachers on that first visit to Wrigley Field for his fifth birthday. The synapses were firing but cognitive explanations were slow to follow.

The first thing Roman did was hire Ryan on the spot to help him build his empire. Then he started buying. A year later, what had once been seen by local children as a stuffy antiques store had become a hub for nerds, geeks, and baseball fans everywhere. Not only had store profits doubled, but Roman found himself at the center of a bustling, raucous, and growing community.

The store was never empty again, and Roman couldn't have been happier.

Which is when I met him. A few years after my dad had died, and reeling from a learning disability that had placed me well behind my peers, I felt lonely and disconnected. I struggled with friendships and couldn't contemplate finding a place where I felt that I belonged.

But then I did.

When I walked into Century's Antiques, I met a group of kids who were just like me. They became my community. We were the outcasts, the nerds, those not popular enough to have their calendar populated with social events and parties. We existed under the benevolence of our "sponsor." Roman always had a kind word, a new pack of cards to give away and open, and some well-placed advice when one of us came in moping over our latest disappointment.

Looking back on my childhood, this meant everything.

Unfortunately, at first glance, the story doesn't have a happy ending. After a couple of years, Roman was diagnosed with metastatic cancer. Exhausted from chemotherapy, and an unexpected strike in Major League Baseball, he saw his record profits begin to spiral down. On a quiet Saturday morning, Roman closed Century's Antiques, leaving a hole in the community felt particularly acutely by a rambunctious group of teens and preteens who had needed somewhere to belong.

Although Roman's days were numbered, those moments behind the counter mentoring the neighborhood kids while sorting through cards and chewing the godawful gum that came wedged between each pack were some of his most joyful. Roman had stumbled into purpose and it led to happiness.

I'm not talking about earth-shattering, world-saving, fame-causing purpose—the kind that people often dream of; the kind that causes anxiety when we're told (or think we're told) we must have it to live a life of meaning and contentment. That's because **the first step to cracking the purpose code is realizing that the purpose that brings meaning and**

contentment *isn't* that kind of purpose at all. It's not *Purpose* with a big, shining capital letter; it's *purpose* with a little "p." Small—but with a bigger, better, more meaningful impact on your life than the grandest imaginable all-consuming *PURPOSE* in bright lights.

This purpose is found in small beckonings to pursue the things we are passionate about.

In Part 1 of this book, we will discuss how to go about finding one's purpose. But for now, trust me when I say that each and every one of us have these callings if we just learn how to listen to them.

Before continuing, there is another point to be made here. While some might say that Roman *found* his purpose, I would wholeheartedly disagree. He didn't find his purpose. He *created* it. He listened to intuition, became intentional, then built the life he wanted to lead. His first step was to hire Ryan, that snarky teenager who opened his eyes about the value of what seemed like a few useless pieces of cardboard.

Then, he had to educate himself on the collectibles market, buy inventory, and advertise to potential customers. Roman's brilliance was that he used his enthusiasm for baseball and knowledge of buying and selling "old" things to create a community—a thriving community that depended on Roman just as much as he depended on it.

I am not the only one who remembers Roman. There are hundreds of kids out there who found their lives in suburban America just a little more bearable and even exciting because Century's Antiques existed. And those kids took that newfound confidence, struck out into the world, and built and created things of their own.

Some—like me—became doctors; others became lawyers, or engineers. Some bought and sold stuff, just like Roman. Others created things that brought people joy or made their lives better. The effects of Roman's sense of purpose, his passion, didn't end when he lost his battle with cancer. Like a pebble dropped into the ocean, his kindness and joy displaced what seemed like an infinitesimally small amount of water. But with nowhere else to go, that water created ripples that spanned the mightiest oceans. It sometimes gained momentum as it joined with other relentlessly small forces to create the largest of waves, and other times receded to become a barely recognizable nudge of water lazily crawling up a sandy beach.

Years later, those kids have grown up and a number have children of their own. And somewhere in a basement, a father and daughter are sorting through an old shoebox and talking about the difference between Topps and Donruss, and the joy of discovery that came with every cellophane pack and the rotten piece of gum that we all ended up chewing anyway.

WHAT THIS BOOK WILL DO FOR YOU

My hope is not only that you can have people such as Roman in your life, but that you can be one of those people too—that you can learn to live out your purpose with passion and joy. To do this, we must remove the stress and anxiety that we so often associate with doing important things.

The disgruntled listener mentioned at the beginning of this introduction was not a mean person, or even truthfully angry when her feelings were fully dissected. Instead, she was *frustrated*. Frustrated by the feeling that there was a grand plan for her that was just out of reach and kept eluding her. In missing this plan, she felt lost, inferior, and even guilty for not living up to what life is supposed to be about or how she was supposed to live it.

I've written this book to help people like you (and her) see that there is no plan other than the one you create! There is no cosmically determined set of activities that will set you free if pursued or damn you for eternity if overlooked. Instead, my hope is for you to find purpose and joy—as Roman did—not in the big and audacious but in the small and intentional activities that you fill your day with. That's where purpose is hiding.

These activities may feel insignificant at times, and they may change from time to time as you grow and evolve. You might find one thing that brings you an overarching sense of purpose, or there might be many. You might create major change immediately in the world around you (like Julia Child), but this does not have to be your intention.

I promise you that if you pursue your individual sense of purpose, regardless of what it is, you will touch lives around you and eventually create a legacy.

Roman is not the only reason I know this. I know it from writing a book about money and purpose and talking to thousands of readers about their reactions. I know it not only from hosting a podcast in which I have interviewed hundreds of thought leaders on how to live a good life, but also from being a guest on hundreds more where I have been pushed to clarify my own thoughts on the role that purpose plays in our wellbeing.

And finally, as a hospice and palliative care physician, I have spent a good deal of my career talking to patients about what has been meaningful for them in life. In extreme cases, I have had some of these conversations with people literally on their deathbeds. As discussed in my previous book, things like making more money and spending more time in the office on nights and weekends are rarely mentioned at that point. Getting that last promotion isn't what occupies people's minds when they are staring down death, surrendering their last ounce of resistance, and accepting the inevitable.

Instead, they think about whether they lived a life that was true to who they are. They question whether they had the courage to be themselves and pursue that which was important to them. They don't spend much time worrying about what they failed at, as long as they think they tried their best.

Living and dying are both about courage. One of our biggest misconceptions is to believe that the balance of courage is saved up for the end. The truth, however, is that it is in the beginning—and especially in the middle—that we need it the most.

Many of you reading this book are in the middle as we speak. Maybe you are struggling to take care of parents and children at the same time and feel like you have lost yourself somewhere in-between. Maybe you are part of a generation that finds itself more educated than ever but with fewer options and less direction than previous generations: all dressed up and nowhere to go.

If you are feeling lost, then this book is for you.

HERE'S WHERE WE'RE GOING

This book is ultimately a journey toward happiness.

There is a longstanding debate on how to define the true meaning of *happiness* and whether it is a goal that we should strive for. Some believe it is a transitory chemical phenomenon; others the holy grail of existence.

Different words are used—*contentment*, *self-actualization*, *wellbeing* (or, as in my last book, *purpose*, *identity*, and *connections*)—but my contention is that, for most of us, the reality remains the same.

We are looking for a healthy sense of peace, belonging, and the hope that our lives make some sort of difference in a world full of randomness.

Here's how this book can help you get there.

In Part 1, we start with the paradox that purpose is both super-important to living a happy life and riddled with stress and anxiety, and show how to resolve this by breaking down purpose into its two kinds: "big P" *Purpose* and "little p" *purpose*. We will discover why the latter is better and more happiness-affirming than the former, and then explore how we can find it in our daily lives. Along the way, we will disprove one of the biggest misconceptions in personal finance today: that money can buy happiness.

In Part 2, we will explore the roles of both meaning and purpose in bringing happiness. While these terms are often used interchangeably, *meaning* actually refers to our cognitive understanding of the past; while *purpose* points us to action regarding our present and future. It turns out that we need both.

I will explore meaning in terms of the stories we tell ourselves about ourselves. Becoming the hero of our own journey makes the past bearable and the future limitless.

I will introduce the powerfully helpful concept of *the climb*: a framework which equips us to build a life of "little P" purpose.

And finally, in Part 3, we will discuss why it all matters. One of the main reasons most people focus on "big P" Purpose is because they think that it is the most assured way to have a greater impact. Big, audacious goals are partly big and audacious because they get people's attention. Many believe that true purpose *must* create either some sort of social good or a large-scale personal improvement. You have to either win the Nobel Prize or become a billionaire.

In fact, long-term, generationally impactful, and legacy-building purpose is *much more likely* to be of the little p kind. In Part 3, we will explain why.

My aim for you in reading this book is to embrace purpose in a different way than you have in the past. I want to provide a kind of purpose prescription to help you crack the purpose code. We will extirpate the stress and anxiety that often come with this topic, and instead help you see it as a wonderful opportunity to learn not only who you are but what you want—and how to make it happen.

Purpose doesn't need to be something glamorous or difficult to find. In fact, it doesn't need to be something you find at all, but instead something you create.

Let's begin the process in which we learn how to create it—together.

PART 1:
THE DUALITY
OF PURPOSE

BIG P   LITTLE P

Cilia was one of the most content people I had ever encountered, even when her beloved mother entered the hospice program. While her trust fund provided wealth, comfort, and ease, it was her charity work that filled her soul. Her parents' successful restaurant chain had not only provided material wealth but led to the creation of one of the largest homeless shelters and food pantries in the Midwest.

Tragic as it may have been, her father's sudden passing from a heart attack a decade prior had done nothing to slow the pace or success of the burgeoning business. While her mother managed both the highly lucrative commercial endeavor and the charitable arm, Cilia was free to spend her days in the shelter, arranging beds, comforting the outcast, and dishing out delicious food to hungry mouths. She was a living monument to the love and legacy that her parents had bestowed on the world when they had generously begun diverting profits to help the local community.

When it came to the business side, her mother's chronic and progressive illness was mostly planned for. The board had already named a successor and the transfer of responsibilities was going even more smoothly than had been scheduled. The goal was to minimize any financial hiccups that might arise unexpectedly.

The pantry and shelter, however, were not as meticulously planned for. Within hours of the funeral and the heart-wrenching afternoon at the gravesite, Cilia was informed by the board that they expected her to take on oversight and possible expansion of the charitable arm of the business.

To say that she felt some trepidation was an understatement. Her father and mother had always managed all the numbers, board meetings, and strategic planning. Cilia's joy and peace remained there in the front office, welcoming the homeless through the doors and providing food and comfort. Her inclination was to stay in the same place. To change nothing.

Yet the board had an even bigger plan that proved to be quite compelling. Over the next few years, new shelters would be opened and the number of mouths fed could be doubled or tripled. A big, audacious goal—didn't Cilia owe this to her mother? Her father? Those in need?

As the years passed, the plans expanded and expanded. Cilia found that she had less time to spend in the kitchen doling out food, as she spent more time in the executive suite talking to donors and discussing the design of each new shelter. She became very good at her new "job," but found that the joy was fleeting. Although she might have been impacting more lives each time a new strategy was set in place, she became overwhelmed with the reality that the more her company expanded, the more pressure she felt to grow to an even greater level.

Cilia mourned not only the premature loss of both her parents, but also the sense of purposefulness that had felt so fulfilling in her younger years. Even though the impact of her daily actions had multiplied many times over after her ascent in her parents' company, she was personally less happy than ever. In fact, it could be said that as Cilia's *purposefulness* increased, her enjoyment of her daily activities and motivation decreased. Can purpose actually become toxic? It did for Cilia; and my bet is that it has for some of you also.

Reading the last few paragraphs, I'm sure many of you are asking: "How could this be?"

As we will discuss in the following chapters, many studies (as well as common sense) suggest that having a sense of purpose is highly correlated with all sorts of wonderful things—health, longevity, and happiness. Isn't that what all the self-help gurus tell us? If we just find the right sense of purpose, everything will be okay. We will be happy and healthy, and the sun will always shine.

Except when it doesn't.

Cilia's story reminds us that purpose is much more nuanced. We see that the search for purpose can be riddled with anxiety and loss as well as joy and happiness. To truly glean all the benefits, we must parse out these different aspects and differentiate between those which nurture us and those which hinder. We must understand the duality of purpose and overcome this paradox. We must crack the purpose code.

CHAPTER 1:
IS PURPOSE A FOUR-LETTER WORD?

What I love most about having my own podcast is interviewing people—I thrive on creating great conversations. I have discovered, however, a line of questioning that's sure to bring the dialog to a screeching halt. If you ever need more uncomfortable silences in your life, all you have to do is bring up the topic of purpose. You're welcome!

My guests love discussing the *what* and *how* of building a prosperous business or lifestyle, but are loath to discuss the *why*. Their faces go blank and they try to transition to another subject. The discomfort is palpable.

Like the audiences I speak to, the question of purpose gets their backs up. If it's doing that for people at the top of their game in business and life, it can do so for anyone.

Many see *purpose* as nothing more than a four-letter word—something one doesn't talk about in polite society.

How can this be?

The scientific evidence is clear: having a sense of purpose leads to greater happiness, increased longevity, and better health. Yet time and time again, I am reminded by my readers and listeners that purpose anxiety not only is real, but often makes people think that pursuing purpose is futile. How do we resolve this quandary?

In this chapter, we will explore the scientific evidence and break down the crucial role that purpose plays in most of our lives. We will dive into the heart of the purpose paradox: the challenge that purpose can be both life-affirming and destructive at the same time.

As the evidence will demonstrate, most of this discrepancy is due to the fact that purpose is not one but at least *two* different entities. How we feel about our sense of purpose, at any given time, likely depends on which definition we are using.

THE JOY OF PURPOSE

I have been privileged to take care of countless people as they battled with terminal illness and ultimately made the heart-wrenching decision to forgo curative treatment and embrace palliative care. I have been at the bedside as my patients took their last breaths. I have heard many deathbed regrets—and rejoiced in the fondest of memories.

Dying tends to clarify one's feelings about life. While I have heard many sad stories, I also have celebrated the triumph of those who die with a sense of peace.

Without a doubt, the most peaceful people I encounter are always those who had a strong sense of purpose throughout life. Sometimes that sense of purpose was projected toward changing the world—like Cilia's story just now. The original idea for the homeless shelter and food kitchen actually came from her mother, Marie, and was inspired by memories of childhood charity with her brothers: the looks on the faces of those they helped, the genuine gratitude they received. Even as Marie succumbed to her chronic illness, those childhood memories—and the new ones she had made with her own daughter from feeding and housing their community—still made her smile.

But you would be mistaken in thinking that only those who set out to change the world can feel such happiness pursuing purpose.

Carlos often proclaimed that you could lock him in a room with a canvas and a paintbrush, and the rest of the world would cease to exist. He died quietly at home in his one-bedroom apartment with little fanfare. Carlos had few friends and not a single living family member. Yet the hospice nurses were surprised how someone who seemed so alone could be so joyful as they visited him at home toward the end. His tiny apartment was full of colorful canvases.

Carlos would get a wistful look in his eyes when the conversation turned to his paintings. He talked about them as if they were his babies. He would amaze his visitors with vivid descriptions of the intention behind each brushstroke. Painting created an unending well of meaning in his life, and Carlos would die a happy man with dreams of what his next canvas could look like.

I have hundreds of other anecdotes about how purpose played an important role in people's lives as witnessed on their deathbeds. Anecdotes, however, only tell part of the story. To really understand the role purpose plays in our lives, we have to dig into the data.

And, it turns out, there is plenty of it.

PURPOSE BY THE NUMBERS

Although my intention is to help you use this book to completely redefine the role of purpose in your life, I think we need to first agree upon the colloquial use of the word. *Purpose*, when discussed in scientific research, generally boils down to some version of the reason we do the things we do. It is the intention behind our actions, why we build and create. It is our *why*. Researchers use the term *purpose in life.*

Given that having a sense of purpose in life is thought to be under our direct control, much scientific research has focused on the effect of pursuing it. And the studies are stunningly positive. So stunningly positive, in fact, that it is worth digging into the numbers to demonstrate how important purpose can be in our lives. The bulk of this research comes from the longitudinal US Health and Retirement Study conducted by the University of Michigan. The study interviews approximately 20,000 respondents every two years on subjects like healthcare, housing, assets, pensions, employment, and disability.

A 2019 study using data from the project in the *JAMA Network Open* looked at the association of purpose in life and overall mortality among US adults over the age of 50.[3] Purpose was measured by a seven-item questionnaire and individuals were given one of five purpose scores based on their answers. The participants were then monitored for the next five years, and health outcomes were tracked. The study concluded that a stronger sense of purpose in life was associated not only with decreased overall mortality but also with a lower risk of dying of heart, circulatory, and blood disorders specifically.

And the benefits are not limited to mortality. A 2021 study, also using the US Health and Retirement Study data, showed that those in the top versus lowest quartile of purpose in life had a 24% lower chance of becoming physically inactive, a 33% lower likelihood of developing sleep problems, and a 22% lower risk of being overweight.[4]

While longevity and general wellness are important, ultimately what we really want to know is whether pursuing purpose in life will lead to greater happiness. While the concept of happiness can be hard to define, several studies have looked at the connection in various populations.

Roback and Griffin studied 118 college students and asked them to fill out a series of purpose in life inventories, depression questionnaires, and happiness scales. They found a strong positive relationship between purpose in life and happiness, and a negative correlation between life purpose and (death) depression.[5] Kaylin Ratner looked at adolescents' daily sense of purposefulness and reported that on days when young people felt more purposeful, they had a greater measurable sense of wellbeing.[6] There is even data suggesting that employees benefit from managers who create a culture of purpose-driven work in the office.[7]

Given all these positives, it feels almost unimaginable that purpose could be anything but beneficial for our overall wellbeing and happiness. Yet Cilia and Marie, the mother and daughter we met earlier, demonstrate that the purpose code can be a complicated one to crack.

Cilia found joy in her sense of purpose when she was checking in people to the homeless shelter and handing out food to the hungry. Marie, on the other hand, almost never showed her face in the actual shelter; she felt her purpose come alive in making the big administrative decisions that set everything in motion, while leaving the details to others.

When, upon her mother's death, Cilia ascended to a larger and arguably more impactful role, it brought nothing but anxiety. Her ultimate goals were the same—they all worked toward the same "purpose"—but the sense of fulfillment from living out that purpose had slipped away. Indeed, serving the same purpose now brought depression and loss of sleep.

What had changed for Cilia were the size of her goals and her daily activities. Instead of concentrating on helping each individual person, as she had previously, Cilia now had grander goals of improving the whole community. She therefore spent far less time behind the counter ladling out nutritious food and far more behind the computer screen drafting grant applications and thank-you letters. Those were the goals of her mother—goals that, unfortunately, were much less gratifying for

Cilia. The *product* of her hard work (improving the whole community) had become more central than the *process* of serving her fellow humans. This felt diametrically opposed to the happiness that both Cilia and her mother had experienced before, when there was a sense of balance or natural compatibility between activity and aim. Their input had felt as meaningful as the outcome.

The mistake of allowing these two things to drift apart can become a death spiral: activities become ever less fulfilling in proportion to the ambition of the goal and the sacrifices needed to achieve it; while the goal becomes ever more ambitious to compensate for the lack of fulfillment and the bitterness of the sacrifice felt in its pursuit.

Purpose becomes panic ridden and stressful—little better than a four-letter word.

Have you ever found yourself feeling like Cilia, daunted by the concept of purpose? Has it ever felt like a weight hanging over your head ready to inevitably topple down on you?

If so, do not fret. You are not alone. You are suffering from what I like to describe as the *dark side of purpose*. It is called *purpose anxiety*. Chances are you have experienced it at least once in your life.

THE DARK SIDE OF PURPOSE

Unfortunately, purpose anxiety is something I am intimately familiar with. In 2014, suffering from horrendous burnout in my role as a primary care doctor, it became increasingly clear that my stamina was coming up short. Overwhelmed and exhausted, I knew that I couldn't stand the idea of working another year—much less another few decades—in this taxing profession.

My discovery of financial independence, and the epiphany that I had enough money to leave my job forever, were exciting at first. I daydreamed about simply walking away from work.

Yet before long, my feelings of joy were replaced with a crushing weight of anxiety. Purpose anxiety, to be more exact. I had spent my whole childhood and young adulthood building a life centered on being a doctor. My big audacious goal was to save lives, heal the world, and make a difference. Years into practicing, sometimes I felt like I was able to achieve that goal.

To step away from medicine was to abandon what felt so near and dear; to step away from my purpose. What would fill the enormous void left behind? How would I create a new identity that avoided all that I had come to hate about medicine, and yet feel every bit as important? My mind went blank, and my mouth went dry. The truth is that I had no clue.

And this gave me earth-shattering anxiety. Anxiety that took years of contemplation, journaling, and even therapy to resolve. From my initial discovery of financial independence in 2014 to my last day in the office was a backbreaking four years. This process might have taken even longer if it was not for being nudged by receiving a summons to court for a medical malpractice lawsuit (which was eventually dropped).

In hindsight, I now think of this period of my life as an immeasurable boon. How lucky was I to be given this chance not only to reevaluate, but also to reinvent myself and my sense of purpose? Shouldn't all of us have this chance at least once in our lifetime? Without question, the answer is a resounding *yes*.

So why do these life pivots provoke so much anxiety?

WHAT AM I HERE FOR?

Purpose anxiety is the fear of not knowing your purpose in life. It was first defined by Larissa Rainey in her sentinel paper entitled "The Search for Purpose in Life: An Exploration of Purpose, the Search Process, and Purpose Anxiety."[8] Her intention was to use the term to encapsulate the negative feelings associated with struggling to find one's purpose in life. These feelings often include stress, fear, worry, frustration, and anxiety.

She found that the great majority of people crave a sense of purpose, and that roughly 91% of them encounter at least some anxiety in their search for it. This purpose anxiety "significantly hampers well-being." Her intention was not to suggest that individuals should try to avoid pursuing the concept of purpose. But, of course, the associated anxiety that she identifies has done just that for many people.

How do you know if you're experiencing purpose anxiety?

It may be harder to realize than you think. Purpose anxiety can manifest in many ways other than clearcut psychological distress. Although we may not be sufficiently in touch with our feelings on the inside, the signs can be obvious when we evaluate our actions and our career paths.

Job hopping, for instance, can be a healthy attempt to increase one's salary and gain much-needed experience. It can also be a manifestation of purpose anxiety. When we focus on finding the perfect job, we may, in fact, be attempting to search for external cues that we are creating internal meaning and joy. In other words, it will never be the job title or salary that will bring true happiness. Those are just labels or numbers. Instead, we should strive to create more fulfilling roles and fill our time with more purposeful activities. Concentrating on a job title or a salary is an awkward attempt to find purpose in place of the more difficult process of creating it. And, more importantly, attaining these new titles often leaves us feeling more empty than full inside, so we again contemplate moving on to the next job, hoping for a better outcome.

Imposter syndrome is another way purpose anxiety plays out in everyday life. We convince ourselves that we are not good enough at what we do. While it is worth noting that this is experienced by many conscientious professionals who are rightfully stretching into a new role, there is also a possible darker side. What may actually be happening is that a role is not truly fitting our internal wants, needs, or goals. We ask ourselves if we are good enough for the job—as opposed to whether the job is good enough for us. We attribute poor fit to a lack of professionalism, when what we should really be questioning is whether being good at a particular job is what we really want.

Another common sign that you are suffering from purpose anxiety is the belief that if you are **having trouble finding your one true purpose, then that purpose must not actually exist**. This, again, confuses finding your purpose with creating it (which we will discuss more in Chapter 3). More importantly, it leads to the errant conclusion that we have one big true purpose instead of many different colors and flavors of purpose with varying intensities. We place so much stress on getting it exactly right that we miss the fact that *perfect* is often the enemy of *good*. There is a lot of room for creativity here. Purpose is truly in the eye of the beholder.

One last sign that you are becoming a victim of purpose anxiety is when you find yourself **playing the comparison game** to the point where it is upsetting you. While it is common to evaluate how you match up to the success of others, it usually creates feelings of insecurity and more instead of less confusion. It heightens purpose anxiety because in comparing, we are ultimately coopting our opinion of someone else's version of purpose and trying to make it our own. The disconnect comes when you realize that each person has their own individual source of motivation and measuring sticks. Instead of trying to fit into another's belt loops, you have to buy your own belt and create your own notches.

By definition, your purpose is unlikely to be the exact same as mine. Why, then, do we keep trying to hold our pants up in the same manner?

IN THE WEEDS

When it comes to the modern world, we are wading in the weeds of purpose anxiety. The challenge isn't merely personal. Purpose anxiety isn't your fault, and it isn't a problem with you. Recognizing what drives it, however, is a powerful tool in avoiding the common pitfalls. While it may be impossible to pinpoint all the reasons that purpose anxiety has multiplied so quickly in today's society, let's take a moment to identify a few of the major contributors.

Longevity

It is estimated that global life expectancy has more than doubled since 1900, topping out at over 70 years of age.[9] We are all living longer than ever.

Imagine being born in a less industrialized country in 1890. Your likelihood of living past the age of 35 was much diminished. Because of this, people simply had less time to worry about purpose. Childhood and adolescence, as well as old age and infirmity, took up a much greater portion of our lifespan.

Wealth

Rapid and overwhelming industrial growth transformed the way we live. It led directly to the formation of not only a wealthy industrial class, but also a prosperous middle class and greater numbers of blue-collar workers. Technological breakthroughs upgraded our options for transportation and the expansion of the electrical grid made it possible for people to better determine their own sleep/wake cycle. Machines replaced a lot of heavy labor, and automation replaced some of the most time-consuming work.

Because of these radical shifts in society, we have much more free time than our forebears. In fact, a recent RAND study estimated that the average American has at least five hours of free time a day.[10]

Even the concept of retirement is relatively new. Not only are most people now getting to *have* a retirement, but the average time spent in retirement in the US has increased by nearly five years since 1970.[11] For the first time in history, we have unprecedented amounts of time to ponder our own existence, with our minds not engaged in the all-consuming task of survival or making money.

Nature abhors a vacuum. The question remains how we will fill it.

Quiet quitters

People have been quietly quitting for years now, detaching themselves from the workplace and building identities unconstrained by what they do for a living. It is now more common than ever to find meaning outside the nine-to-five instead of within. Automation, outsourcing, and a trend away from the old archetype of the "company man" have made the average worker feel less connected and responsible for the company mission.

Your job is just not that into you. So why should you be into it?

The unintended consequence is that our jobs—once a significant source of purpose and even enjoyment—are no longer providing either.

But work is not the only place people are quietly quitting. They are also abandoning religion at an ever-increasing pace. According to Jason Derose, who writes for National Public Radio, the importance of religion in the lives of Americans is shrinking.[12] He points to the fact that in a recent Public Religion Research Institute study, just 16% of Americans surveyed said religion was the most important thing in their lives, down from 20% a decade ago.

People are no longer finding purpose in work or religion. They are rejecting the large external structures that previously created a general framework for meaning. Lacking these external guideposts, they instead become experts at the comparison game—and social media influencers are happy to target those needy eyes and attention spans.

Social media and the comparison game

No wonder we are suffering serious anxiety: we have chosen to define purpose in life based on unattainable and often unrealistic standards flashed in front of our eyes each time we gaze down at our phones.

Subliminally we are being told that purpose looks like nice clothes, hard bodies, and frequent trips to Europe. These things, for most, unfortunately, are just flat-out unattainable. We lack the money, fashion sense, genetics, and willpower. Furthermore, when we invest so much in social media, we are trying to steal someone else's sense of purpose instead of doing the difficult work of defining and building our own.

And it is making us miserable.

CHASING TREADMILLS

The question is how to successfully maneuver through this landscape—to move beyond the weeds and to achieve (and bask in the glow of) all the positive longevity and happiness effects that have been proven to come with a meaningful life.

After much research and work in this area, I believe there is a simple but fundamental change that can accomplish almost all of this. Inevitably, however, that isn't where human nature tends to start.

I'll always remember Ricki, a middle-aged hospice patient who was an exceedingly successful lawyer. He started his career as a paralegal in a small firm and earned enough money to fund law school. When he graduated, the job market was horrible, and he was forced to go out and practice on his own. As the years passed, Ricki piled on the achievements.

He went from a small firm to a large firm. From sole partner to lead partner of over 100 other lawyers. From a small player in the Chicagoland area to one of the largest firms in the country.

With every step forward and accomplishment, he felt a surge of pride. However, weeks later, the shine of each new benchmark began to fade, and Ricki would invent bigger and more audacious goals to shoot for. In fact, even as he lay dying of an unexpected kidney cancer, he propped his computer on the bedstand and worked mercilessly away on a new deal to sell his firm for one of the largest sums ever recorded for such a transaction.

While conducting a life review (a process of life evaluation we will delve deeper into in Chapter 3) with Ricki, a hospice nurse uncovered a startling discovery. Ricki was exhausted. He didn't particularly like being a lawyer and only cared about the current negotiations regarding the firm insofar as they would facilitate a record-breaking sale.

Yet Ricki had been chasing these accomplishments all his life.

He had become a victim of the **achievement treadmill**. The short-term exultation of success fueled his heroically pumping legs, but he could no longer divine the next awe-inspiring destination. He kept running and running but was getting nowhere. He was never happy or truly fulfilled. His joy was always short-lived until he had worked out the next goal to accomplish.

When we focus on big audacious goals that often have little personal meaning, we find that there are three main possibilities—none of them good:

- We fail to achieve our goal. This creates a sense of never fulfilling our purpose and we reach the end of life bitter and regretful.
- We achieve our goal but instead of feeling thrilled, we feel empty. We spent our time doing things we didn't like because we thought the outcome would feel purposeful—but hedonic adaption is cruel when it comes to fulfilling goals. When people realize that the air is no better at the top of the mountain, instead of asking *why*, many just find a bigger mountain to climb.
- Upon spending an inordinate amount of time and energy achieving that which we craved, we become panicked that we will lose it. The

stock market will go down and our net worth will falter. A new and better law firm will come along and kill our market share. This fear—loss aversion—can often be doubly as terrifying as the possibility of never achieving our goal in the first place.

———————

We began this chapter by asking whether purpose is something of a four-letter word. The answer is obviously no—plenty of studies show that purpose in life can lead to greater longevity, health, and happiness. Yet anxiety associated with finding meaning is not only real, but rampant in today's society. As demonstrated in this chapter, there are many reasons why.

All too often, we make one of two bad choices at this point.

We either give up on purpose, the way the conference goer that I described in the introduction did; or we chain ourselves to never-ending treadmills that do very little to fill our souls.

The key to cracking the purpose code is to realize that neither of those choices will bring us what we are looking for—to extract all the good associated with purpose and leave all the anxiety behind. The only way to do this is to recognize that purpose, in its simplest form, is not one but two different entities.

We'll meet these two very interesting entities in the next chapter.

A PURPOSE PRESCRIPTION: PERFORMING A SOCIAL MEDIA AUDIT

- Clear your schedule for an hour on two separate occasions in the next week. If you can, turn off all electronics or silence your phone. Find a quiet place where you will not be disturbed.

- Turn your smartphone back on and open your favorite social media app.

- Set an alarm for ten minutes and browse your favorite app in the way you would on any given Saturday morning after reaching for your phone on your bedside table upon waking up.

- If you are the type who goes down a rabbit hole and reads full articles ... don't! Limit yourself to 30 seconds on any individual post and then move on.

- Upon hearing your ten-minute alarm go off, power down your phone and take a few deep breaths. Center yourself and relax.

- Now concentrate on two or three images or stories that stuck out to you—specifically, images that caused FOMO (fear of missing out) or that felt particularly inspiring or purposeful. Was it a friend's recent vacation? A new fashion purchase by an influencer? A goal weight or body fat percentage boasted by a gym mate? A career milestone of a colleague?

- For each of these goals, realistically calculate the amount of time, energy, and resources it would take for you to achieve something similar.

- Would you enjoy the time and energy spent on achieving this goal? Would it be worth your effort? What if, at the end of your journey, you came up short? Would it still have been worth it? Would you feel regret that you had "wasted" your time?

- Finally, imagine if, after achieving this vaunted goal, a new and better goal presented itself. A better car came to market. Or your office mate got an even better promotion. Or, after achieving that target net worth, the newness faded. Would you still be happy? Would the work you had done still feel like it was fulfilling a sense of purpose?

- It's okay if the answers are not clear. The aim of this exercise is to ponder whether goal-oriented purpose—especially other people's goals coopted from social media—is truly the path to living a more meaningful and happy life. In my humble opinion, the answer is definitely *no*. To understand why, let's move on to Chapter 2.

CHAPTER 2:
WHY THE SIZE OF YOUR "P" MAKES ALL THE DIFFERENCE

Searching for your sense of purpose should lead to more happiness and less anxiety, not the opposite. It should not have to be a paradox. Yet time and again, we find that purpose can be complicated—not only for regular people like you and me, but also for those who appear to be at the height of their accomplishments.

From the 1930s to the 1950s, Hedy Lamarr—arguably one of the most successful and well-known actresses in the world—starred in 25 films. She was at the pinnacle of her career, garnering fame and fortune and lauded for her unparalleled beauty. Yet she found herself unfulfilled.

"My face has been my misfortune," she wrote in her 1966 autobiography, *Ecstasy and Me*. "It has attracted six unsuccessful marriage partners. It has attracted all the wrong people into my boudoir and brought me tragedy and heartache for five decades."[13]

Hedy had found that her big audacious sense of purpose—being a starlet—was leaving her burned out and unfulfilled. When asked what made a good actress, her response was: "Any girl can be glamorous. All you have to do is stand still and look stupid."

Hedy, in fact, was anything but stupid. She became so dissatisfied with acting that she spent her time in her trailer between takes and stayed up all night at home enthralled by a completely unrelated activity. She eschewed her previously outsized dreams of fame and fortune for something much more modest but even more fulfilling.[14]

She wanted to be an inventor.

Over the next several decades, Hedy would work on a number of projects—everything from effervescent cola tablets to helping to streamline Howard Hughes' racing airplane. In fact, a patent she held for a "secret communication system" which used "frequency hopping" to guide radio-controlled missiles underwater was adopted by the military and (controversially) has been called a precursor to Wi-Fi.[15]

Hedy never meant to change the world with her inventions. It was the thing she loved doing most. Although her Hollywood producers did their best to hide her intellectual acumen (which they felt would detract from her reputation as an ingenue), she eventually was posthumously inducted into the National Inventors Hall of Fame in 2014 for the development of her frequency-hopping technology.

So how did Hedy get the concept of purpose so right and so wrong at the same time?

In this chapter, we will describe how we fundamentally misinterpret the concept of purpose. We think of it as a single entity. My hope is that you will come to see that it is exactly the opposite. In order to crack the code, we must realize that purpose comes in at least two sizes and your future happiness depends on picking the right one.

Choosing wisely will make all the difference. It will determine whether you live a life full of anxiety and frustration or health and happiness. But make no mistake: you have to choose. Only you can decide what size "P" will fit you best.

I'll give you a hint: the answer is the same for everyone.

THE UNFULFILLED DOCTOR

It's not surprising that I suffered from burnout and eventually left the practice of medicine. Only in retrospect can I see clearly that I had built a life around the wrong-sized purpose. The signs were there along the way, but I chose to ignore them. The reasons are many, but the outcome was always the same. I spent much time thinking about the destination and very little about the path I was taking to get there. That path was much less gratifying than I hoped it would be. I simply didn't enjoy being a doctor.

I had failed to recognize that **the destination *is* in fact the way**, and the path is more important than its end point. I was doomed to fail from the beginning.

These shortcomings started from a very young age. Somehow, as young children often do, I decided that my father's unexpected death was my fault. As silly as it sounds, this belief drove me to coopt his purpose in life. His dream was to delve deeply into medicine and help people, and I felt that I could undo the existential tragedy of his death by taking his place. It was only decades later, while skimming through some of his medical notes left over in my mom's attic, that I realized how different we truly were.

My dad had an innate love of the delicacy and intricacy of the human form and how it goes wrong. I didn't. He thought in extremely three-dimensional terms and was an excellent photographer. I had a learning disability and would often draw words upside-down and backwards. Conversely, I loved deep conversations, and baseball cards, and writing poetry. My father had no interest in those things.

Becoming a doctor totally fulfilled my father's sense of purpose and he loved the moment-to-moment work required to accomplish the goal of helping his fellow man. Unsurprisingly, even when things got tough, his deep interest and love carried him through. Trying to fix the cosmic tragedy of his death, I saw the end goal of helping my fellow man as laudable; but I was actually ill-suited to the day-to-day activities required to meet that goal.

Don't get me wrong: I was able to overcome my discomfort and eventually do exactly as I had planned—walk in my father's shoes. But the blisters that formed on my heels in doing so never callused over. They festered and bled until the pain eventually became unbearable.

I was not made for such work. So why did I keep on pursuing it?

Have you ever found yourself in the same position? Floundering to live someone else's dream and finding that it really doesn't suit your goals and abilities? You realize that instead of enjoying the journey, you are loathing the path and praying to make it to the destination. If this is your current situation, then you—like I was—are lumbering toward burnout. And even becoming that which you strive for is unlikely to make you happy. It certainly didn't for me!

It was not just in the beginning, but even as I continued on my path toward medicine that I realized something was wrong. While I shared some of my colleagues' dreams of having "MD" after my name, I found myself shying away from talking about it with other people. I felt almost embarrassed to tell them what I planned to do for a living. I felt an inexplicable sense of shame.

That shame multiplied even after I began to practice as an attending physician. While my friends and schoolmates were so proud of their profession, I secretly daydreamed about becoming an esteemed writer instead. And the most joyful part of my day was almost always the few minutes I squirreled away to escape my job and work on my blog or some other creative project.

The problem was that I never saw writing as an important enough or viable way to earn a living. Helping people and becoming a doctor ... now *that* was the type of purpose that sounded meaningful to me! I made the mistake back then that many of you are likely making today: I thought that the *bigger* the purpose, the more gratifying it would be to pursue it.

It took many years and quite a bit of emotional heartache to reach the conclusion that I hope to convince you of now: **when it comes to purpose, bigger is not better.**

THE FALLACY OF "BIG P" PURPOSE

From this point on, we will talk about purpose as two separate and distinct entities. For the rest of the chapter, I will demonstrate how most of our anxiety actually stems from what I call **"big P" Purpose.** This is the same kind of purpose that led not only to my yearning to become a doctor, but also to Cilia's certainty that she could take her mother's place and run the family charity, and Ricki's belief that he would find happiness just as soon as he accomplished his next major achievement in law. Big P Purpose is overly focused on outcomes.

"Little P" purpose, on the other hand, is the true creator of the wonderful health and longevity benefits that all those researchers have proven with their studies. It focuses not on the destination or the outcome, but rather on the path or process. Because of this, it lacks glamour. It is even considered downright unsexy. And most people do whatever it takes to avoid this petite purpose in favor of doing something they believe will be more substantial.

Why do we do this?

Before getting into a much more granular discussion about what defines the different types of purpose, I want to theorize on why we are programmed to pursue big P Purpose and eschew little P purpose. Why do we fall for this fallacy?

We all Want to be Unique, Just Like Everyone Else

In the United States, we place a premium on being unique. I suspect some of this comes from the rugged individualism of frontier times. The idea that we should be doggedly individualistic and rely on nothing other than our own ingenuity has predominated in American culture. This ethos persists despite growing wealth, the taming of the environment, and increasing social support.

Instead, we focus on uniqueness: the idea that each of us is special, and that this specialness will set us apart in important ways. Indeed, when we use the term *unique* today, what we are really talking about is success. You are not truly supposed to be different; you are supposed to be better. Build a better widget, accumulate more wealth, reach success at a younger age— that is, unfortunately, what being unique has come to signify.

Steve Jobs wasn't unique. Many of us dream of building and promoting the next technological advance. He was just better. Michael Jordan wasn't unique in dreaming of dominating the basketball court (millions of kids around the world do). He was just better. Oprah Winfrey wasn't unique in building one of the most successful media empires in the world. She was just better.

What we really crave is not just to be different, but to be exceptional. This exceptionalism has built its way into our culture and permeates every aspect of our lives, including our psyche.

Go big or go home.

Why would it be any different for purpose? Why shoot small when you can shoot big? We are taught from an early age that it is not worth doing something unless you do it right. But what if you like doing the thing even if the end result is not what everyone else thinks it should be?

If You Can Dream It …

"If you can dream it, you can do it." This quote—incorrectly attributed to Walt Disney—sums up the ethos of much of modern-day America. All you have to do is have big dreams to eventually do big things. Right?

Yet there are many people who dream of being Michael Jordan and have none of the skill, ability, or genetic attributes (e.g., height) to get there. No matter how much you want to be an inventor or businessperson, you might not have the intellectual capacities. And if your dream is to be the first human to time travel, at present, it seems your wishes will go unfulfilled.

The problem with such messaging is that it places too much importance on big audacious dreams of challenging tasks instead of being thoughtful about what actually fits a person's personality. Not everyone has to hit a home run every time at bat—and, more importantly, most people will fail if that is their intention. Not everyone's purpose needs to be outsized.

Ironically, the true source of the quote is a woman named Sheralyn Silverstein, who created the copy as part of a recruiting tool for General Electric (GE) to convince more young students to "follow their passion" in math and science and eventually work for GE.[16] She wasn't telling kids to become astronauts or neurosurgeons. Her message was much more mundane: become an engineer and help our company make more money.

You are No Better than your Résumé

We define ourselves more by our accomplishments than we do our passions. Furthermore, we are more likely to cling to those things we are good at than those we love.

You can test this hypothesis. Go up to a stranger at a party and ask them to describe themselves. Take note of whether they mention their job, their awards, their education, and their skills. Also take note of how much they emphasize their passions, their relationships, and their personality traits.

Then go look up their résumé online. My bet is that most of things they end up talking to you about could be found in the first few paragraphs of their résumé in one way or another. The bigger and more impressive the accomplishment, the larger the role it will play in both résumé and conversation.

Here's the kicker: according to Zippia, at least 30% of people admit to lying, or at least "bending the truth," on their résumé.[7]

QUESTION: HAVE YOU EVER LIED ON YOUR RESUME?

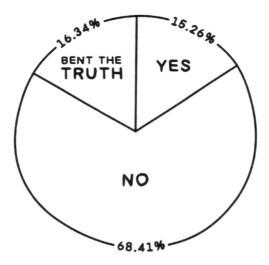

Not only do we reduce ourselves to what we believe are our most consequential work-related bullet points; many of us lie while doing it. I imagine the numbers are even more damning than this report suggests, given the data was taken only from those who would voluntarily admit to their own underhandedness.

We lie because we want our résumés to look more consequential and impressive. We want to convince the world that we are pursuing purpose with a big "P," and we have the accomplishments to prove it.

PURPOSE WITH A BIG "P"

As you can see, there is a relentless pressure both internally and externally to devote our energies to big P Purpose. This pressure ends up creating more anxiety than joy. In fact, I often hear my dying patients complain that they spent too much time on their big audacious goals, to the detriment of their own happiness and the enjoyment of what they already had.

There was Toby, who dreamed of becoming a US senator but could never muster enough campaign funds or support. While dying of Lou Gehrig's disease, he lamented that he had never run for the local school board—a job he might have enjoyed just as much, and which would have been much more attainable.

Or Shanelle, whose designer makeup line almost made it onto *Shark Tank*, but got axed in the last round. Suffering setback after setback, she made barely enough money to subsist. Yet when she became bedbound from multiple sclerosis, she realized that all too often, her true joy had not been in the boardroom, but out front with customers, helping unconfident women feel good about how they looked. She wished she had spent more of her precious time engaged in those types of activities.

Using these examples as a template, along with those of Cilia and Ricki, we can start to get a feel for the characteristics that define big P Purpose. First and foremost, it is goal oriented, as opposed to focusing on process. Whether it be building ten more homeless shelters or securing venture capital funding from a bunch of television stars, this type of purpose often depends on an all-or-nothing equation. You either succeed or you don't. You are either the biggest law firm grossing the highest revenues in Illinois or you are not.

The bigger the goal, the easier it is to fail. These types of goals often rely on some mix of luck, timing, and good genetics. You have to be the right person, at the right time, in the right place. Unfortunately, for most of us, the stars do not align precisely when necessary.

We will likely not cure cancer, become a billionaire, or produce the next mass-consumed item to hit the market. And that's okay. For better or worse, most of us are bound to fail. Toby did. So did Shanelle. Meanwhile, the anxiety that comes with such goals defining our purpose robs us of any enjoyment there might have been in the process of their pursuit. And it defines that process as worthless when the opposite might well be true, for all sorts of reasons.

The other problem with goal-oriented, big P Purpose—as mentioned in Chapter 1—is that it is fleeting. While you can be engaged in an enjoyable process for years (like Cilia while she was handing out food to the homeless), the newness of a major accomplishment is only felt *once*. And once attained, the excitement of gain is replaced by endless worry over its loss. Even if Toby had eventually made it to the Senate, he could always have been replaced in the next election.

Because of these shortcomings, it becomes obvious that when you embrace big P Purpose, you are actually embracing a scarcity mindset. Success has a narrow focus and often comes at the expense of others. There can only be one most successful law firm in each state or county. *Shark Tank* can only accept so many candidates.

Big P Purpose turns out to be pretty small minded.

HOW TO EMBRACE ABUNDANCE
WITH LITTLE P PURPOSE

Up to this point, I have given far more examples of what I consider to be the wrong kind of purpose to pursue. Only Roman—the antiques dealer from the Introduction who changed the world by selling baseball cards—has exhibited anything like the little P purpose that we are going to talk about now.

This has been intentional. The toxic type of purpose is just so much more relatable. It is, in fact, the easiest purpose to decide to pursue. It means meeting society's expectations and following in the footsteps of the herd. The harder decision by far is to do the internal work to find what really lights you up—to discover what can be the basis of a life of true fulfillment. And then you have to find a way to pursue it in the world.

This all takes effort but will prove more than worth it.

We will explore how to do that in greater depth in Chapter 3. First, we need to get a complete picture of what little P purpose truly is.

Little P purpose embraces an abundance mentality. There is room for everyone—I mean everyone—to pursue that which brings them inner joy and happiness. This pursuit will never rely on whether someone else is succeeding or failing. It will never be limited by some resource that another human being has already gobbled up.

Little P purpose is a process-oriented purpose that is impossible to fail. It is associated with health, longevity, and happiness.

Little P purpose centers on you as an individual. It is truly unique in the sense that, while many other people may have your same sense of purpose, how you fulfill that purpose and which activities you choose in pursuing it are all your own. Cilia chose to pursue her little P purpose by spending her days doing hands-on work in the shelter. Marie, her mother, found the same joy in attending board meetings and having coffee with donors. There was room for both.

Abundance.

Little P purpose doesn't deny or detract from the joy of setting and achieving goals; it just doesn't depend on them.

This type of purpose is concerned much more with the process involved and much less with the product. Those who enjoy the benefits of little P purpose immediately win because they enjoy doing an activity regardless of whether anything comes of it. Roman thrived on selling baseball cards and building a community. The work itself lit him up. The side effect of running a successful business was a happy accident. If he hadn't made enough money from the baseball cards, he would still have sold them, and just derived more of his income from selling antiques.

When we focus on little P purpose instead of big P Purpose, we move the locus of control away from chance or other people and back into our own hands. If I read a book about billionaires because of my love of studying historical figures and enjoy each chapter, story, and conclusion, that book will be well worth my time regardless of whether it helps me become a billionaire or not.

Although we can choose what activities to fill our lives with, we can't always choose the outcome. **Because of this, little P purpose is anything but all or nothing. In fact, it is all or all. There is no way to fail.** And if you find these activities no longer fulfilling, there is no reason whatsoever not to do something else.

Little P purpose espouses the idea of **incremental change**. It recognizes that humans like the idea of progress. We enjoy setting goals and even surpassing them at times. The trick is that the smaller version of purpose focuses on incremental gains which are in our power to achieve. Shanelle could have used her love of helping people to reach out more in her community. Instead of *Shark Tank*, she could have spent her time and energy slowly building her customer base, learning how to leverage their support. She would have found this process much more gratifying.

And finally, little P purpose recognizes that people, as well as what they find meaningful, can change. Unlike big audacious goals that take years or even decades to achieve, the small, more personal types of purpose are ongoing projects that are enjoyable regardless of the outcome. If one activity or purpose no longer feels like it fits, we can easily pivot to something else. We haven't wasted any time, energy, or money. Now, this is not to say that we haven't *used* any time, energy, or money—we surely have. But we were doing things that we enjoyed the process of doing.

That was our purpose, and we followed it. And we felt the benefits.

What if, instead of focusing on where we want to be in five years' time, we instead meditate on what experiences we want to have? What projects do we want to be involved in and what do we want to be doing on any given Monday morning? Changing this focus will ground us in the here and now.

The ultimate outcome of focusing on little P purpose is that people have fewer regrets when they die. Instead of wishing they had achieved that which they didn't have the energy, courage, or talent to pursue, they can point to many daily activities that brought them joy and created meaning. Remember Carlos from Chapter 1, who would get into deep conversations with his hospice nurses about the joy of painting? It is true that his works may never have hung at the Metropolitan Museum of Art or been auctioned off for millions of dollars. On his deathbed, however, Carlos could celebrate the fact that he had spent most of his days doing something deeply meaningful.

If you found out you were going to die tomorrow, could you say the same thing? Why not? Have you incorporated little P purpose into your life?

I'VE EXPERIENCED BOTH

The skeptic in you is undoubtedly questioning my theory. You are asking how I am sure that pursuing little P purpose yields all the good effects while chasing big P Purpose ends in anxiety. I don't blame you. I would be doing the same thing. Unfortunately, the scientific evidence of this just doesn't exist yet. It may one day. But in the meantime, we are left to rely on common sense. Deep down, we all intuitively know what stresses us out about purpose.

The other resource we have, of course, is our stories. And besides relaying what I have learned from my hospice patients, I have also spent a great deal of my own life pursuing big P Purpose. It was only when I found financial freedom that I allowed myself to pivot toward looking at purpose in a completely different way. That way was, of course, little P purpose.

Here is how I came to it.

As mentioned previously, I spent the first 35 years of my life building a sense of purpose around dreams of practicing medicine. This was a big audacious goal. It started around the age of seven, after my father died. Did I come to this idea of purpose because I had a life-changing experience with my own doctor, had an inclination for science, or felt a pressing need to help people? Unfortunately, the answer is *no*. I decided that I wanted to become a doctor because it is what my father did. It was my own juvenile belief of how to right the wrong of his premature death and all the poor patients he left behind.

I broke the first cardinal rule of purpose and coopted the purpose of someone else: my father. I cannot say that there wasn't joy in the journey. I truly enjoyed my academic life and thrived in settings where I could help other people. I gained insight into the human condition and had a sense, initially at least, that I was doing something that changed people's lives.

The joy, however, was short-lived. As the stress of being a doctor became more severe, a relentless and overbearing sense of burnout set in. I was exhausted and couldn't find a way out of the life I had created. This wasn't a feeling that came on suddenly. It grew for years. I developed other interests that I had to squeeze into the minutes and hours between doctoring. I found time to write and prepare for public speaking at lunchtime and after my wife and children had gone to sleep.

The disconnect began early on in my career. I made few friends in medical school and often was loath to let strangers know what I did for a living. I felt more shame than pride at the moniker my peers were so proudly bandying around; I had no interest in identifying myself as a physician.

Looking back, I had clearly fallen into the big P Purpose trap. I was living out my father's purpose. I had chosen a big ambitious goal of helping people—so big, in fact, you could never complete it—even though the process of achieving that goal was no longer fulfilling me. I didn't like going to work every day and seldom enjoyed the process.

When I realized that I was financially independent, I tried to turn making money into my sense of purpose. I became the victim of a completely different kind of treadmill, and thought that I would enjoy the process of doctoring more if I exchanged the goal of helping people for the new goal of achieving an ultra-high net worth.

None of these attempts made me happy. Far from it. I fell into a deep depression and began having panic attacks. This at a time when I had enough money to do pretty much whatever I wanted. But money could not fill the hole I felt in my soul. Neither could those old trauma-induced dreams of becoming a doctor and changing the world.

Eventually, I realized that if I wanted to learn how to be happy again, I had to start from scratch and build a life centered on what would fill me up. I realized that there were these inklings, these callings, that I had been ignoring my whole life. In my most secret of secret dreams, I was a writer, publishing my most intimate ideas and leading deep and meaningful conversations. These were dreams that never focused on an end goal or an accomplishment, but instead were deeply immersed in **the joy of doing**.

Given the boon of financial independence, I slowly began to build and integrate the life that I dreamed about. I blogged, then podcasted, and eventually wrote *Taking Stock*. While I would be lying if I said that I didn't have some hopes or expectations of preferred outcomes, I can honestly say that the process of doing these things created a sense of serenity that I had never felt before. Of course, I wanted millions of people to listen to my podcast and read my book; but this time my happiness no longer depended on it.

I took control of my sense of purpose and made sure that when I did get the itch for incremental improvement, it was the type of goal that I had some sort of control over. Maybe I couldn't get 100,000 more listeners to download my podcast episode every month, but I surely could study up on how to become a better interviewer.

These changes felt transformative. I began to realize that purpose was not something that was set in stone, that I had to mold myself around; but instead that purpose could spring forth from my internal vision of how I wanted to spend my time.

Wouldn't you rather define your purpose instead of your purpose defining you?

I have tried both and I find the former much more appealing. I believe that you will too. The first thing required is to recognize that you may also have become a victim of big P Purpose. The solution then becomes crystal clear: relinquish the victimization and start to build a life of little P purpose to replace it.

"How do you find little P purpose?" you may ask. We will discuss this important topic in the next chapter. But first, let me give you a hint.

You don't find little P purpose; you *create* it.

THE RULES OF PURPOSE

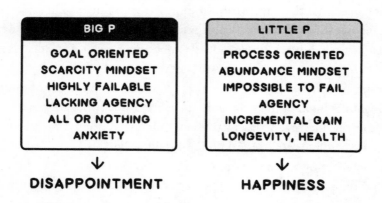

BIG P	LITTLE P
GOAL ORIENTED	PROCESS ORIENTED
SCARCITY MINDSET	ABUNDANCE MINDSET
HIGHLY FAILABLE	IMPOSSIBLE TO FAIL
LACKING AGENCY	AGENCY
ALL OR NOTHING	INCREMENTAL GAIN
ANXIETY	LONGEVITY, HEALTH
↓	↓
DISAPPOINTMENT	HAPPINESS

A PURPOSE PRESCRIPTION:
PERFORMING A PURPOSE AUDIT

- Clear your schedule for an hour on two separate occasions in the next week. If you can, turn off all electronics or silence your phone. Find a quiet place where you will not be disturbed.

- Turn your smartphone back on, open the Calendar app and focus on all the activities scheduled for the last week. If you have a paper or other form of calendar, no worries—feel free to pull that out instead.

- For each entry over the last seven days, assign a broad category to describe the purpose behind that activity (e.g., "Hobbies," "Making a living" (i.e., "Work"), "Family fun"). Limit yourself to five or six categories and don't worry if one activity fits into several.

- Using the criteria established in this chapter, see if you can connect each calendar entry to a big P Purpose activity or a little P purpose activity. Think about the difference between goal-oriented activities and things you enjoy the process of doing. Do these activities feel driven by an abundance mindset or a scarcity mindset? Is failure a possible outcome? If you never achieved your goal, would you still be glad you were engaged in this activity?

- Take a deep breath. This is not meant to be easy or clear cut. Sometimes you will not be able to categorize an activity neatly. Once finished, tabulate what percentage of your time is being taken up with big P Purpose versus little P purpose. Is the balance lopsided on one side or the other? Are you surprised by the tabulation?

• It's okay if this exercise feels uncomfortable. It is meant to make you question how you are spending your time. Is this week representative of your last year? Of your last decade?

If answering these questions has made you realize that you have less little P purpose in your life than you would like, get ready to do some hard work. In Chapter 3, we will discuss how to go about changing the balance to create a more satisfying and fulfilling life.

CHAPTER 3:
YOU CAN'T FIND WHAT ISN'T LOST

In December 1938, Nicholas Winton, a self-absorbed stockbroker, did something that was both out of character and would change the trajectory of his life, as well as that of many others. He said *yes* to someone he normally would not have said yes to (a technique we will later refer to as the "spaghetti method"). On a simple impulse, he canceled his skiing trip to Switzerland, at the behest of a friend, and booked a flight to Prague to aid refugees in Czechoslovakia (which had just been annexed by Germany).

Over the next month, Nicholas risked life and limb to establish a program to transport unaccompanied Jewish children out of war-torn areas before the Germans could capture them. In the nine months leading up to World War II, he helped transport 669 children from Czechoslovakia to Britain.

Nicholas, like many of us, had no grand plans when he discovered his purpose. He hadn't set out to change the world or gain notoriety. He later recalled: "I never thought what I did 70 years ago was going to have such a big impact as apparently it has." And: "Every child saved with my help is the justification of my existence on this Earth, and not a title to glory."

Following the war, Winton worked as a banker and continued to create a life of purpose by participating in various charitable organizations. In fact, his efforts largely went unrecognized until 50 years later, when his wife found a scrapbook in their attic in 1988 detailing his all but forgotten work.[18] His dedication to helping others was later acknowledged and he received numerous awards and honors, eventually being knighted by Queen Elizabeth II in 2003.

Like Sir Nicholas, some of us are lucky enough to happen upon our purpose in an unexpected way. If this is not the case for you, however, there is no reason to feel distress. It turns out that average, everyday people like you and me can identify these important purpose anchors and build a life every bit as fulfilling as that of Sir Nicholas.

Sarah, for instance, had written me, frustrated after reading my book *Taking Stock*. While she wholeheartedly agreed that she should be pursuing purpose in order to live a more meaningful and happy life, she felt in a rut. Like so many I had come across in the personal finance world, the closer she came to resolving her money issues, the higher her anxiety rose. It was so much more comfortable to worry about money. Building wealth was a finite problem with answers that could be divined through reading books, searching the internet, and listening to podcasts.

Purpose, however, felt infinite. Which meant there were so many ways to fail. So many ways to strike out. In the brief months she had been contemplating this, she could feel depression creeping over her. To stem that, she did what she often did when she needed answers to difficult questions: hopped on Instagram and browsed through posts by her friends and favorite influencers. If purpose was to be found, it would certainly reveal itself there. Or maybe on Tik-Tok?

After many failed starts, Sarah was more frustrated than ever. Her super-successful ex-roommate from college was selling jewelry on Etsy and tweeted about her first five-figure month of sales. Sarah went out and bought a bunch of beads at the local craft store but found that her interest waned after a few days.

One of her favorite influencers had just posted pictures of a luxurious trip to Italy. Inspired by the idea of travel, Sarah scoured travel websites in consideration of an extended trip or slow travel expedition. But she quickly realized that, logistically, leaving home would be difficult. She had her dog to take care of, and she loved babysitting for her three-year-old niece whose parents could certainly use the help. Did she really want to be absent during those formative years? She had always dreamed of being the cool auntie.

Feeling like the internet might not be the best place to find actionable inspiration, she turned to friends and family. She remembered that her last mentor at work had quit the year before to become a campaign manager for a local politician fighting for social justice, better maternity and paternity benefits, and solutions to global warming. These were things Sarah truly cared about.

A month later, after volunteering every Wednesday with the campaign, Sarah found herself more discouraged than ever. Instead of being on the frontlines fighting the good fight, she spent most of her time making fliers and calling potential donors, who often hung up the phone before she could even explain why she was bothering them. If this was purpose, maybe she didn't want to pursue it after all.

Sarah found herself more confused than when she started. And a lot more depressed. No matter how hard she looked, she couldn't find her purpose. It eluded her at every turn. She couldn't understand why it seemed so easy for everyone else, yet so opaque for her.

Sarah, it turns out, was making a common and predictable mistake when it comes to purpose. **Unlike the big audacious goals we try to steal from other people, little P purpose is created and not found.** The difference is subtle but important. We create this type of purpose by concentrating on that which fills our souls, and then being intentional about taking action.

In this chapter, I will help you answer the sometimes-stifling question: "What fills my soul?" Unlike in Sarah's previously described attempts, we will not look externally but rather turn an eye toward our own internal wants, needs, and joys. While many people may share the same sense of purpose, how we live out that purpose often depends on our own individual likes and dislikes.

In the pages that follow, we will turn the infinite into the finite by concentrating on your internal desires instead of letting others' vision of purpose cloud your judgment. To do this, we will begin with an old hospice technique called the **life review**. Used to help dying patients find peace on their final journey, I have found that it can be a great clarifier for those who still have a long life ahead of them yet need to rediscover joy and passion in their daily activities. After that, I will share a number of other techniques that will hopefully fan the flames of the hidden fire that burns within you.

Let's start with the life review.

CONDUCTING A LIFE REVIEW

The concept of a life review was introduced by Robert Butler in an article in the periodical *Psychiatry* in 1963.[19] Butler, a noted gerontologist and the first-ever director of the National Institute on Aging, studied the needs of the elderly—both those who were healthy and those with dementia. I first learned of his review technique from the amazing social workers in the hospice community. It is commonly performed by nurses, chaplains, social workers, and even doctors.

A life review is simply a structured list of questions that helps people assess the important moments and themes in their lives. It also touches on regrets. Here are just a few sample questions you might find in one:

- What has been your greatest success in life?
- What has been your greatest failure?
- Name a moment or period in your life when you were happiest? What made this so?
- When did you feel the least in control of your life? Why?
- Who are the people who have had the greatest influence on you?
- What relationships have caused you the greatest pain? What happened to the relationship?

I will stop short of providing a full life review questionnaire here, but you can get a flavor of the technique from the questions above. You will find a more exhaustive list of life review questions at the end of this chapter.

The benefits of a life review have been well demonstrated. They include not only decreased anxiety, but a plethora of other positives. For instance, Liu and fellow researchers showed that conducting a life review with elderly patients nearing end of life significantly decreased symptoms of anxiety and depression, while also elevating mood and an overall sense of wellbeing.[20] Another study looked at the effects of life review on a non-terminal aging population.[21] It similarly found a large reduction in depressive symptoms and an overall improvement in wellbeing.

While these studies don't necessarily prove that conducting a life review will be as meaningful in a younger population, there are several reasons to believe that it will. William Damon, writing for *Psychology Today* in 2021, enumerated some of the benefits:

- an acceptance of the events and choices that have shaped our lives, reflecting gratitude for the life we've been given rather than self-doubt and regret;
- a more authentic (and thus more robust) understanding of who we are and how we got to be that way, reflecting the highly developed, reassuring sense of self that psychologist Erik Erikson called "ego integrity"; and
- greater clarity on the direction our lives should take going forward, reflecting what we have learned from our experiences and the purposes that have given our lives meaning in the past.

He further points out that the ability to look at the past in an open and honest way helps us better understand our present values and future aspirations. Indeed, it is these future aspirations which bring us back to how conducting our own life review can help us create little P purpose today. It means not only enumerating regrets of the past, but revisiting what was magical and awe inspiring. This may be the first time you look appraisingly at your childhood and young adult life, and begin to question what deeper wants and needs drove your behavior and overall sense of contentment.

How can we reclaim that which we abandoned due to lack of energy, courage, or time? Conducting a life review will allow us to use what we found meaningful in the past as a template to build a better present and future.

It certainly did for Sarah. After reading her email, we spent an hour on Zoom rehashing her unsuccessful and frustrating attempts to uncover a path toward purpose. Upon finishing our call, I left her with what she felt would be an agonizing homework assignment. I encouraged her to conduct her own life review. I provided her with a bunch of helpful links to peruse and checklists to follow, and hoped that she wouldn't let her current state of discouragement keep her from doing this important exercise.

Horses.

A single word was the title of Sarah's email almost a month after our conversation. She had finally got around to conducting her life review. Although it took several hours over multiple days, she eventually overcame the discomfort of answering these difficult and often emotional questions, and stumbled upon an epiphany.

Her fondest memories of childhood always centered around horses—whether it was drawing them as a young child or riding them as a teenager. She felt most at home and safest hanging around the stables. In fact, she had spent more time thinking about horses than almost anything else until she left for college.

Then, inexplicably, she forgot about them. She became busier at university and no longer had time to return home to ride. Her career aspirations flourished into an interest in journalism, and often her summers were spent on internships in cities around the country. After leaving college and landing her first job, she had daydreamed about finding a stable outside the city, but there never seemed to be enough time. *And have you seen how much it costs nowadays to stable and care for a horse?!*

Two decades later, in better financial shape than ever but struggling as an editor for a fashion magazine that rarely held her interest, Sarah had her first inkling of that small, quiet kind of purpose.

The kind of purpose that could sustain her for a lifetime.

SEPARATING THE BABY FROM THE BATHWATER

When I realized that I was totally burned out in medicine and also financially independent, I could have slammed the door on medicine and never looked back. I could have walked into my practice manager's office and told her to "take your job and shove it!" But I didn't. I didn't throw the baby out with the bathwater for one simple and basic reason: I had no idea what I wanted to do with my life.

I spent my whole childhood and young adulthood identifying as someone who wanted to be, and would eventually become, a doctor. This had been the main purpose of my existence. Realizing that I had chosen wrongly left me with a terrifying purpose vacuum: "If I'm not a doctor, what am I? If my purpose is not to care for and heal my fellow man, what is it?"

If you have ever been in a position that makes you fundamentally question your previously held sense of purpose and identity, you know how utterly disorientating such thoughts can be. You might not have the courage to tear everything down to the studs and start all over again. I certainly didn't. So instead, I did the next best thing.

I began the process of **subtraction**. I sat down with a pen and pad of paper one day and wrote down all my rules and responsibilities as a physician. I included every job description I had, and every title I carried. It took a few days, but eventually I ended up with a fairly detailed job description.

Then, I grabbed an extra-sharp pencil and started slashing away. Every category that caused me pain and distress—I slashed it. Every chore that I dreaded so much that I didn't want to get out of bed in the morning—I slashed it. Every meeting I had signed up for or committee I had been assigned to but was an overall waste of time and energy? You guessed it—I slashed it. In fact, I slashed so much, with a demonic look in my eyes

> The **art of subtraction** is the process of removing things from your life that no longer serve you.

and sweat pouring down my cheeks, that I finally slowed down enough to recognize that the paper was totally filled with haphazard slashes except for one lonesome corner with a barely readable entry.

Hospice.

I loved the small part of every month devoted to hospice. It was the only part of my job that still brought me joy. While sitting with my hospice team, I no longer felt the overwhelming weight of being a doctor. I was just a regular person using whatever skills and knowledge I had to make a difference. And I loved this feeling.

Suddenly my sense of loss no longer felt so great. I would do hospice work no matter what I was paid for it. I would do it for free. I would do it because it felt like part of the purpose I was put on Earth to fulfill. Not a big audacious purpose that would change the world, but little daily activities that made me feel connected to my own abilities as well as my hospice team, and those patients that were so badly in need of help.

I had found my anchor.

In much the same way, Sarah also found hers. Conducting the life review helped her remember her sense of connection and joy while spending time at the stable and taking care of horses. This was a beginning. As beginnings go, though, she still had much work to do. She was still weighed down by a job she didn't love. Knowledge and action are two different things. She now had knowledge of something that felt like purpose in her life. What action could she take to start living a life more in tune with this discovery?

My next homework assignment for Sarah was to practice the art of subtraction when it came to her work environment. Was there anything about the job that she still liked? That still felt purposeful? What was her favorite task?

Sarah had fallen out of love with the fashion industry and generally couldn't care less which colors were in this season and which were not. She liked some of the mechanical tasks when it came to bringing the magazine to press each month, but not enough to sustain her. After making nearly as many scribbles on her pad of paper as I had on mine, there was one task that she absolutely would never have gotten rid of had she had the choice.

Years previously, Sarah had been given the task of collecting a series of stories for a new section of the magazine. Unlike the hardcore industry tips and tricks that made up most of each issue, this section was a humorous retelling of real-life fashion foibles submitted by readers. Sarah couldn't help smiling as she remembered working with the authors on editing their submissions, often dissolving in a puddle of laughter.

It was the one part of her job that she truly loved throughout all those years of soul-sucking tasks. But just like that, the ever-popular section was shut down when a new chief editor took over and felt that the stories were not serious enough. Sarah was crushed then, but elated now. She had not just one anchor to build purpose around in her life—horses—but also a work-related activity that she would choose to do even if she wasn't being paid for it.

Sometimes we get so anxious about searching for purpose that we forget that we might have created it already somewhere in our lives. I challenge you to look at what you spend most of your time doing—even those things that you say you loathe. Are the embers of a flame hiding in plain sight?

Maybe they need just a wee bit of oxygen.

THE WISDOM OF CHILDREN

I don't think we need to belabor Sarah's story any further for you to realize that recalling the passions of your childhood is a quick way to remind yourself of what lights you up. While the life review tangentially touches on this technique, I feel it is still an important exercise on its own because childhood is a magical time in our lives.

Young children simply don't have as much purpose anxiety. They have not yet become victims of *coulds* and *shoulds*. They have not yet been told what they could or should do, so they have complete freedom to dream openly and freely. We indulge young children and often tolerate—and even encourage—their crazy antics. As a seven-year-old, when I told my mom I wanted to build a swimming pool in the backyard, she didn't tell me I couldn't do it. She happily helped me clear the leaves as we spent an afternoon giggling away.

It is only as we get older that the adults in our life, and society, start placing restraints on our dreams. My mother would have told the teenage me that I was daffy to want to build my own swimming pool in the backyard. There are city ordinances, and the cost of labor, and permits, and liability, and, and, and ... The list goes on. Older kids are quickly put in their place and discouraged from thinking outside the box—as well as filled to the brim with societal expectations.

Parents tell kids that they should become doctors or lawyers, not journalists who love horses and like to edit humorous stories. The advertising and marketing gurus tell us what we should look like and what products we should buy. We are told to conform to standards that all too often mimic another's version of purpose or are meant to line some business's pockets.

In the process, most of our childhood dreams and loves are crushed. But when looking to create purpose in our lives, this is fertile ground. It is how I became reacquainted with my love of sports and baseball cards. As discussed in the Introduction, my mentor from the antiques store played a big role in my life. But that was only half the story. Part of the reason I loved the store so much was my joy in collecting—a joy that consumed huge amounts of my childhood.

At some point before going to college, my passion waned. Not because I loved collecting any less, but more likely because in society's eyes, I had outgrown such childhood interests. College meant putting the nose to the grindstone and concentrating on what I thought was my only true purpose: becoming a doctor.

Years later, my eye still catches anything to do with baseball or collectibles. Even though I haven't watched or followed the sport in years, they are the first stories I read if I pick up a magazine or newspaper. I realized that baseball cards are probably a great place for me to go back and start practicing what I preach about little P purpose.

What aspects of your childhood have you left behind? Could they be the spark that rekindles a long-forgotten flame?

THE SPAGHETTI METHOD

There are several other techniques to identify little P purpose in our lives that I will briefly touch on in this section. The first, which I often reference in my talks, is to pay attention to the crazy ideas and inspired moments that pop up in the most inopportune times. Almost everyone I know has, at some point, stayed up half the night because they were so inspired by an idea that they couldn't go back to sleep. Their mind twists and turns, and finally they drag themselves out of bed the next day exhausted and head out to a full day of work.

The **"spaghetti method"** describes the process of trial and error when it comes to purpose.

Unfortunately, that is usually the end of the story. As the day goes on, those magical thoughts of the night before start to feel too grand or ephemeral—just not realistic. We convince ourselves that we were being overly exuberant and go back to our boring, mundane lives. The idea dies.

How many times has this happened to you? I've done this very thing several times in the last few years. But what if we paid attention to those crazy ideas? What if we took them seriously? I do believe that this is our subconscious urging us to pursue that which is really important. It is very possibly true that the idea may be off the wall, and all but impossible to accomplish. But the fact that we got excited enough to forgo sleep should be an indication that there is the kernel of something exciting and meaningful there. Why not explore these wacky ideas?

What do we have to lose?

If you find yourself still struggling even after trying all the techniques we have discussed up to this point, it is time to call for some help. The first and easiest solution is to ask family and friends. Sometimes they see you in ways you can't see yourself. Occasionally they have insights that can truly change your mind. Although Sarah had no idea what spurred a sense of purpose in her life, you know who did? Her mother. All her mom had to do was look around at the countless boxes of leftover belongings from her childhood bedroom which were overflowing with equestrian trophies and drawings of horses and riders.

One caveat to bringing your loved ones into this discussion is to realize that the exact opposite can also be true. Your family may see you through a lens of their choosing, and not your own. They may have limiting beliefs based on who they think you are or should be. That is why it is especially important to always make sure that what they tell you chimes with who you know yourself to be. If the people in your life tell you to pursue activities that don't feel right, trust your intuition.

If family can't provide the answers, it might be time to bring in the professionals. Although this may be a therapist or social worker, many different types of life and career coaches are also available. These professionals can ask probing questions and help you not only reorganize but reinterpret your current situation. Sometimes they are even provided as a perk in the workplace. Other times, as with a therapist, your meetings may be paid for by health insurance.

Do your due diligence. Make sure that any career or life coach is credentialed (there are various methods and credentialing agencies) and check out their references. The best references are personal, so look around to the happiest, most successful and well-adjusted people you know. Do they use anyone? And if so, can you get their names and numbers?

Up until this point, I have suggested methodical techniques to draw out a hidden sense of purpose that is sitting there waiting for you. I recognize, however, that these techniques may not yield results. Maybe you never had any childhood dreams or middle of the night moments. Maybe conducting your own life review brings you no closer to deciding what you want in life. If this is the case, there is one more technique to try.

The spaghetti method.

That's right: throw a bunch of spaghetti against the wall and see what sticks. This is a shotgun-oriented trial-and-error process. Open yourself up to the universe and see what happens. This means saying *yes* to people and activities that you normally wouldn't say *yes* to. It means stepping into the discomfort of the unknown and new, and allowing yourself to occasionally look foolish.

Although vulnerability is never easy, if you are thoughtful and authentic, good things will follow. By using the spaghetti method, you are embracing vulnerability, then taking stock of the experiences afterward. The magic happens when, after several new experiences, you feel an affinity toward one or two of them. Then it's time to really dive in. Explore those affinities and say yes to even more related opportunities. Which of these activities bring you a sense of joy and fulfillment?

IF YOU BUILD IT, THEY WILL COME

Using the techniques in this chapter, you can begin to formulate what little P purpose can look like in your life. That's the good news. The bad news is that you now actually have to create the life you want to live. You don't find purpose; you create it. You will hear me say this over and over again.

Roman didn't find purpose through selling baseball cards—he recognized the affinity and then spent a lot of time learning the trade and building the community. In the same manner, Sarah is now way ahead of the game. She identified her love of horses as an anchor, and she remembers that there were parts of the publishing business that she still likes. Yet, as I discussed with her during our last virtual meeting, the work has just begun. Now she has to create meaningful activities surrounding these things that bring her joy. The possibilities are limitless:

- She could take horse-riding lessons.
- She could work on the weekends in a stable.
- She could apply to magazines that focus on horse racing or on humorous narratives.
- She could start an equestrian blog or podcast.

Anything is possible if you are willing to play an active role and create a life full of activities that you love to be involved in. Although this may require some difficult and uncomfortable work, the payoff is well worth it. As we will explore in depth in Part 3, the point of all we are discussing is even bigger than little P purpose. When you engage in these types of activities, you gain something even more important: community and connections. This is the prize awarded at the end of all this struggle. You will create communities that help you learn and grow.

If you build it, they will come. If you are authentic and intentional about living a purposeful life, you will attract to yourself likeminded individuals who will nourish and support you. There are no shortcuts when it comes to this most important activity. There are no cheat codes. This form of happiness can't be bought, no matter how much money you have.

Or at least, that is what I am going to try to convince you of in the next chapter.

A PURPOSE PRESCRIPTION: PERFORMING A WORK AUDIT

- Clear your schedule for an hour on two separate occasions in the next week. If you can, turn off all electronics or silence your phone. Find a quiet place where you will not be disturbed.

- Although this exercise can be done electronically, it is best to start with a standard-sized piece of white printer paper and a sharpened pencil.

- Separate the page into three distinct columns. Write down all the rules and responsibilities of your current job in the first column; your most common work activities in the second column; and the names of the people and the organizations you frequently interact with in the third column.

- Pause for a moment and take a good look. This is an inventory of your current work life. Does it seem overwhelming? Positive? Negative? Purposeful or lacking purpose? There are no right answers here, so feel free to allow your mind to ponder these questions unhindered by what you think the answers should be.

- After no more than five minutes, take out that sharp pencil and start slashing away. Put a line through each entry that feels useless, annoying, anxiety provoking, or particularly loathsome. Only leave those activities that bring you joy, that feel particularly purposeful, or that you would do even if you weren't getting paid for them.

- You have now engaged in the art of subtraction when it comes to your current employment. Look hard at what is left pristine on the paper. Is there anything untouched? Did you obliterate everything? Is there anything about your job that you would keep if you suddenly had more money than you could ever need?

- There are no right answers here. In the search for little P purpose, it often makes sense to clearly evaluate how you spend your time before taking a sledgehammer to the temple you have so meticulously built. You ended up in your particular job for a reason. Does that reason still exist?

- The entries that remain untouched are a good starting point or anchor for creating your new sense of purpose.

- Don't be discouraged if your whole piece of paper looks like one big scribble. It just means that you may have to use some of the other techniques that we mentioned in this chapter to probe further.

- If, on the other hand, the sole standing entry has to do with your income or salary, it is definitely time to move on to the next chapter. Because, unfortunately, while money can buy many things, happiness is not one of them.

Life Review Questions and Resources

Below is a list of life review questions by category (modified from Continua).[22]

Reflecting on childhood:

- Can you share your earliest memories?
- Describe your childhood experiences.
- Who were your primary caregivers and what were their personalities like?

- Describe your siblings and your relationship with them.
- What is your fondest memory from your childhood?
- What important lessons did you learn during your early years?
- How would you describe your family's economic status growing up?
- What were your favorite games and recreational activities?
- What were some of your family traditions?
- What was your favorite toy as a child?
- Describe your school experiences.
- Did you have any pets growing up?

Navigating adolescence:

- What are your most vivid memories from your teenage years?
- How would you describe your personality during adolescence?
- What expectations were placed on teenagers during your time?
- Describe your school and the education you received.
- Who were your closest friends in your teenage years?
- Describe your relationship with your parents during adolescence.
- Did you have any role models, mentors, or heroes?
- What chores were you responsible for as a teenager?
- When did you start dating? Share memories of your first date and first kiss.
- Describe your first job and your earnings.
- What challenges did you face as a teenager and what did you enjoy most?

Embracing adulthood:

- Share your experiences from your twenties and thirties.
- Did you get married? What attracted you to your partner?
- Describe your children, if you have any.
- How would you describe yourself during this stage of life?
- What hobbies and interests did you pursue?
- What role did money play in your life during this time?
- Describe your career and professional experiences.
- Who were your closest friends as an adult?

- What challenges did your family face?
- Share your favorite memories from this time in your life.
- What major historical events impacted you the most?

Growing older and wiser:

- What challenges and joys did you experience during your middle adulthood?
- How did these experiences shape your perspective on the world and your way of living?
- What accomplishments are you proudest of?
- Do you have any regrets or unfulfilled dreams?
- What do you consider your greatest successes?
- How has your life met, exceeded, or fallen short of your expectations?
- Do you practice any faith or spiritual traditions?
- Can you share some defining moments from your life?
- What advice would you give to your children and grandchildren?
- Do you miss any aspects of the "good old days"?

Life review resources:

- Continua life review questions: tinyurl.com/continualifereview
- The case for regular life reviews: https://www.wellandgood.com/life-reviews-live-without-regrets/
- The connection between purpose and a life review: https://www.psychologytoday.com/us/blog/the-puzzles-your-past/202107/purpose-and-the-life-review
- Jane Fonda and Oprah Winfrey on doing a life review: https://www.oprah.com/own-oprahshow/jane-fonda-reveals-how-to-do-your-own-life-review-video

CHAPTER 4:
MONEY CAN'T BUY LOVE, PURPOSE, OR HAPPINESS

Dietrick thought he'd finally found the answer to all his problems—and there were a lot of them. He hated his computer programming job and rarely had any sense of joy in his daily activities. All he wanted to do was finish work as fast as possible in order to escape the office and relax at home. Exhausted by his soul-crushing nine-to-five, he generally passed out on the couch in front of the television (though not before ordering Uber Eats). His waistline was a testament to inactivity as well as his discontentment.

Discovering the financial independence movement seemed to solve all his problems. All he had to do was save up enough money and invest wisely. This would lead to a net worth high enough to quit working altogether.

It was as if the sun—all of a sudden—had come out from behind the clouds. Dietrick's daily work activities became almost bearable. Almost. As the money in his bank account increased, he had to admit that a few of the programs he was creating had real value. According to his calculations, he would be financially independent when his net worth was equal to 25 times his yearly spending.

Although this felt difficult at first, a mix of spending cuts, intentional saving, and wise investing made quitting his job a real possibility in just a few short years. By this time, Dietrick had found a group of other people with similar interests and had even gone to a financial independence conference. He updated his spreadsheets every week and tracked the stock market daily. These activities gave his life a sense of meaning. For the first time in years, Dietrick felt totally connected.

So much so, in fact, that even upon reaching his financial independence number, he stayed on at work an extra six months just to be sure. His office mates threw him a party to celebrate his early retirement. Dietrick could not have been happier.

This joy lasted all of a few months. That was precisely how long it took him to work through his Netflix queue, master most of the shoot 'em up games he was obsessed with, and take that long-dreamed-of trip to Italy that he had never had time for.

The problem, Dietrick realized, was that money had solved one specific thing. It had relieved him of the responsibility of showing up each day to a job that he didn't particularly love.

Robbed of that responsibility, he found himself more confused than ever. He had never really contemplated what would bring him joy other than escaping that which he loathed. He had never, for a moment, contemplated any sort of purpose other than making enough money to be free.

This freedom is highly sought after by many who feel that money and wealth are the keys to wellbeing. But can money really buy happiness? This age-old question continues to be debated in new and exciting ways— as we'll soon see.

Those who believe it *can* often point to the life-changing effect of giving someone without basic food or security enough income to cover such things. Yet many lottery winners end up destitute and unhappier than before they bought their first lucky (unlucky?) ticket.

In this chapter, we will delve deeper into this urgent question of whether money can buy happiness—and what the answers say about purpose. As you might have guessed, there is much data, both scientific and otherwise, on the subject.

YET ANOTHER PARADOX

As with the concept of purpose, the relationship between money and happiness is paradoxical—the evidence points to two opposite conclusions.

In order to understand these conclusions, we first need to define some of the terminology used by researchers while discussing happiness and its relationship to money. In the studies we are about to discuss, there are generally two terms that are used. These were initially defined by Daniel Kahneman and Angus Deaton in their groundbreaking research article from 2010.[23] They defined *emotional wellbeing* as how you feel on a daily basis—what we commonly refer to as "happiness." *Life evaluation*, on the other hand, is a person's long-term sense of accomplishment or satisfaction.

Kahneman and Deaton originally reported an analysis of more than 450,000 responses to the Gallup-Healthways Well-Being Index—a daily survey of 1,000 US residents conducted by the Gallup Organization. They found that income and education were both closely related to life evaluation; while health, caregiving, and loneliness were more associated with daily emotional wellbeing. Furthermore, they found that while emotional wellbeing increases proportionately with income, the effects top out at $75,000 a year. After that, there is no benefit.

They concluded:

> More money does not necessarily buy more happiness, but less money is associated with emotional pain. Perhaps $75,000 is a threshold beyond which further increases in income no longer improve individuals' ability to do what matters most to their emotional well-being, such as spending time with people they like, avoiding pain and disease, and enjoying leisure.

Not to be outdone, Mathew Killingsworth studied the same phenomenon but found no threshold level of income or flattening of the happiness curve.[24] Eventually both groups of researchers collaborated to further refine their hypothesis. They concluded that money could increase happiness in already happy people; but for unhappy people, the effects eventually attenuated as income rose.[25]

In other words, money can buy happiness for some people, but for others only to a point. These findings are hard to interpret for people like Dietrick. Maybe he should keep working and accumulating more wealth. Could he be one of the lucky ones?

Unfortunately for Dietrick, as well as the rest of us, the waters get even muddier. A recent study questioned whether the best way to increase wellbeing in low-income countries is to stimulate economic growth. The conclusion was rather shocking. The writers found that in communities with the lowest levels of economic development, citizens reported a degree of happiness comparable to that found in Scandinavian countries (which typically rate highest in the world).[26]

One of the reasons this may be true is a phenomenon referred to as the "Easterlin Paradox." This states that at any given point in time, happiness and income are directly correlated among people and nations; but over the long term, these two indices are no longer significantly related. The principal reason why is suspected to be social comparison.[27] Income makes us happy when it contrasts with those who are less fortunate than us. Apparently, the opposite is also true: a rising tide lowers all ships. In other words, economic improvements across large populations have little effect on overall happiness. Dietrick will be happy as long as his income or net worth is measurably better than those of his peers and neighbors.

The **Easterlin Paradox** is the theory that at any given point, happiness and income are directly correlated; but over the long term, they are no longer related.

Finally, a last piece of the puzzle came from Aaker et al in their groundbreaking work published in the journal *Emotion* in 2022.[28] They found that although happiness may increase with wealth in general, as income levels go down, meaning and purpose are much stronger predictors. This association was found not only in the United States but in large-scale datasets spanning more than 500,000 people from 123 countries across six continents.

So how do we explain this? More money makes us happier except past a certain level, and definitely not in poor countries or places where everyone equally enjoys the same economic boon. And furthermore, as income goes down, it is meaning and purpose rather than money that predict happiness. What the heck is going on here? How do we use this information to better understand the Dietricks of this world and better find contentment?

Our first task is to recognize that there is a difference between *correlation* and *causation*. In other words, Kahneman, Deaton, and Killingsworth may indeed be correct that wellbeing is *correlated* with happiness. That, however, is a far cry from saying that one causes the other. It may be that, *a priori*, happy people are better at making money or earning a higher income. Or that in less economically developed countries, showing signs of happiness is frowned upon. There can be many explanations of why two characteristics are associated with each other, rather than that one causes the other.

CROSSING THE CORRELATION-CAUSATION DIVIDE

In order to cross the correlation-causation divide, we have to search for a stronger, better type of evidence. Instead of studying two separate characteristics and then assuming that their relationship is meaningful, we could start by studying people before and after a change in one characteristic and then measure a difference in the other. This is called a prospective study when the outcomes are monitored in real time, and a retrospective study when we look backwards to reconstruct and analyze data.

For many experiments, we can purposefully introduce a change and then note the outcome. For others, such as a change in wealth, we can monitor people after a drastic change has happened to them (instead of introducing it ourselves) and then measure the differences.

This is a neat way to cross the correlation-causation divide.

Unsurprisingly, some of this work has been done already. A famous study by Brickman compared lottery winners and paraplegic accident victims many years after their life-changing events.[29] Astonishingly, they found that the lottery winners were unhappier than expected, and the accident victims were happier. They attributed these findings to habituation—we tend to return to our previous baseline. A more recent study confirmed these findings after studying 400 lottery winners from 1988-2011 in Sweden.[30] While there might have been some benefit in overall life evaluation, their sense of overall happiness or wellbeing was not statistically different.

A prospective study that has been ongoing for decades has continuously asked some of these important questions about the identifiable contributors to happiness. The Harvard Study of Adult Development started in 1938 and followed 724 men from various economic and social backgrounds from their teenage years onwards.[31] Researchers asked the participants to fill out questionnaires every two years on the subject of emotional and mental wellbeing. They even interviewed family members and loved ones.

The results of this very long-term study were shocking. When it came to happiness, it was not money, achievement, career choice, exercise, or a healthy diet that made respondents happy. **It turned out, after 85 years of studying, that one and only one thing was a strong predictor of overall happiness: positive social relationships.** Those who felt more connected to others lived longer and happier. Period.

If this is sounding familiar, you may recall that we ended the last chapter by discussing how the real reward at the end of the game of life is community and connections. This is the true goal of purpose.

WINNING THE GAME

When we take into account all this data, our advice for Dietrick becomes very clear. Although higher incomes and greater wealth have been correlated with higher levels of emotional wellbeing and a better sense of life evaluation, the results are probably not as relevant on a personal level. For any given person, accruing more wealth likely does not make them happier. It didn't for the lottery winners or for the participants in the Harvard Study.

What is increasingly obvious is that happiness most likely relates to our interactions with other people. This is clear from the Easterlin Paradox. At any given point, higher income may make us happy when compared with those less fortunate. But over the long term—especially if the divide in wealth doesn't grow—the effect habituates and we eventually return to our original happiness baseline. This effect feels relatively negative. It smacks of superiority: one group is deriving pleasure from being more fortunate than others.

In contrast to the Easterlin Paradox, the Harvard study points to a much more important conclusion. The phrase "positive social relationships" is just another way of saying "community and connections." When it comes to happiness, it is our interactions with other people that lead to winning the game. Not as a way of comparing, but in the form of companionship and camaraderie. We feel fulfilled when we help people and are helped by them. When we nurture others and are nurtured by them. When we smile and laugh and teach and learn.

It is a virtuous cycle. Happiness leads to more meaning and purpose. Purpose leads to community and connections. Personal connections and social relationships create more happiness and longevity.

A VIRTUOUS CYCLE

Our recommendations for people like Dietrick thus become rather obvious. Amassing more wealth or increasing his income will make him no happier than quitting his job. Because of hedonic adaptation, he will become habituated to any effect of these economic ups and downs. Research makes it clear that if Dietrick wants to improve his sense of happiness, he needs to create a greater number of enduring social interactions.

Dietrick could pursue these by going to social clubs, spending more time with family, or joining an online dating community. While these would help him become more involved with his fellow human beings, I think there is an easier solution.

It's called "little P purpose." By pursuing a sense of purpose, Dietrick will most likely interact with likeminded people who encounter him in his most authentic and intentional state. Whether learning to rock climb, racing boats across Lake Michigan, or joining the local historical society, his actions will bind him to others who share his passions. He will sometimes be a student and other times a teacher. He will share his joys and his discouragements.

You'll be glad to know that Dietrick's story has a happy ending. He eventually realized that, while he hated his computer programming job, he rather enjoyed computer programming itself. Instead of going back to work for a faceless corporation, he joined a collective of programmers and hackers dedicated to solving software issues for struggling small businesses. His work introduced him to others that shared his passion for complex problem solving. He was constantly challenged to solve larger and more difficult problems that often kept him up in the middle of the night, enthralled and tapping away on his keyboard. He became a mentor to some of the younger volunteers in the collective and even learned a trick or two from the more experienced members. On Friday nights, they all got together at a favorite bar in town for happy hour.

Ultimately, neither wealth nor financial independence made Dietrick happy. Purpose did. Not the overwhelming type of purpose that changes the world, but the small, quiet kind that makes you friends with colleagues and helps people in need. Purpose did something that all the wealth in the world had not been able to do up to that point. It connected Dietrick to other people. People he eventually came to love.

DIETRICK AND I SHARE
THE SAME STORY

I spent the first 40 years of my life without having many connections or community. I could never exactly figure out why. As a kid, I rarely felt like I fitted in at school or in social situations. I left high school with a few friendships, but no real bonds based on shared interests or values. I went to a Big Ten college but had no interest in sports or school spirit. While my friends went to football games on Saturday mornings, I was in the law library studying.

While I was excited about the prospect of becoming a doctor, I didn't necessarily feel a sense of fellowship with my fellow premedical students. In fact, I mostly avoided them. The same carried into medical school. I made very few lasting friendships. When outside in the world, I was extremely reticent to tell people that I was training to be a doctor. I thought, at the time, that was because I didn't have the degree yet. Or that I didn't want to be boastful.

There was very little improvement in residency or as a practicing physician. I didn't like to hang out in the doctor's lounge or identify myself as a physician to people outside the profession. The only doctors I seemed to bond with were those who I met as part of the medicine social media community. These were mainly bloggers who shared the same passion for writing and social activism that I had.

I rarely questioned my isolation. I knew many people who had deep and profound social connections, but I couldn't explain why I was not like them. I figured that I was antisocial or, better yet, too busy to form stronger bonds. After I got married and had children, I convinced myself that my family were all the community I would ever need.

My isolation might have been lifelong if I hadn't learned about managing my own personal finances. The ability to leave my job created the kind of purpose vacuum that I have mentioned in previous chapters. I first tried to fill this vacuum with wealth. I thought that if I could just accumulate enough money, I could not only escape medicine but also be happy. I blindly believed that wealth would lead to this happiness. Although I found ways to accumulate more and more, it led to neither joy nor connections.

I just became an unhappy person with a lot of money.

Eventually I was forced to take stock of my life. I had more money than I would ever need and a job that was supposed to fulfill me, yet the vacuum persisted. None of this felt like purpose to me. Eventually I started to listen to the little whisperings I had long silenced. I began to do some of the exercises in the last chapter and took a long, hard look at my childhood. Overwhelmed by the stress of my daily routines, I started to work the magic of subtraction on my medical practice as well as my life.

All this deep thinking helped me realize that there was a sense of joy buried under all the stress and responsibilities. There were two activities that stood out. Two anchors: hospice and writing. These were the things that I would do even if I wasn't being paid for them. Dreams of writing woke me up in the middle of the night and wouldn't let me fall back asleep.

I bet Dietrick would say the same about creating a unique piece of code.

I threw myself into blogging about personal finance and signed up for various conferences and get-togethers. Not only did I build a number of connections online, but my joy eventually stemmed from people who I met in real life. I realized immediately that I felt closer to my fellow bloggers and writers within minutes than a few of my doctor "friends" who I had known for more than a decade.

I was both relieved and mortified. Relieved that there wasn't something wrong with me and mortified that I had been hiding all these years. Instead of being an introvert, I had just never met anyone while intentionally pursuing any real modicum of purpose. As a doctor, I was constantly hiding from an identity that never suited me very well. Because of this disconnect, my relationships were superficial and I shared little in common with those I was trying to bond with.

Years later, I am living a life that I could have never imagined while being an actively practicing physician. I have friends who I have not only collaborated with but visited in faraway places. I have regular meetings and conferences that I go to, and often meet with collaborators and mentors. My schedule is full of activities I have chosen, and I enjoy almost every single one of them.

I now have a community. I am connected to people in a deeper and more natural way than ever before. I am living out the conclusions gleaned from the Harvard Study of Adult Development. I learned from experience that no matter how much money I had accumulated in the past, no bank account or investment returns ever made me feel as whole as the new friends that I have now built a community with.

I am happier today than at any other time in my life—and none of it cost a single cent.

YOU'RE DOING IT WRONG IF ...

You're doing it wrong if, like Dietrick and me, you think money is the solution to your problems. Money only solves money issues. Happiness is rarely a simple money issue. I think we all know this deep down inside, but sometimes it needs to be said out loud. If we become crystal clear on this issue, however, we can also recognize that spending money can in some circumstances make our life better. There is nuance here. Using money as a tool to offload the chores and responsibilities that don't serve you can have a very positive effect. Accumulating it rarely does.

You are doing it wrong if you think that a lack of money is keeping you from pursuing your sense of purpose. The internet is vast and the resources available with just a few clicks are unquantifiable. You can learn about anything, explore anywhere, and connect with anyone. Free online resources are available for almost any type of knowledge. One minute you can be voyaging down the Grand Canyon in a barrel, the next exploring the differences in grading a rare silver dollar as fine versus very fine. This vast ability to connect has also led to the creation of lean startup businesses. Unlike in the past, you can become an entrepreneur with next to no money.

This is especially true if you are young and feel trapped in a job where you are forced to work long hours just to make ends meet. While money may be one of the tools you are lacking, you may have other tools at your disposal that you are failing to recognize. Young people often have energy, free time (without kids or a mortgage), and passions and communities to exploit. Use these tools to build purpose in your life and you may find that economic opportunities follow. The lack of money should not hold you back.

You are doing it wrong if you are playing the wealth comparison game. Keeping up with the Joneses—whether that concerns your bank accounts or your material belongings—will always end in disaster. First, there will always be someone who has more than you. You are unlikely to be at the very top of the pile. And second, the joy of comparison wears off unless you are continually widening the gap: we tend to fall back to our baseline level of happiness. The bottom line is that the monster always needs to be fed. The treadmill is never-ending. You are bound to tire out and fall off and break your leg.

You are doing it wrong if you are constantly moving the goal line—if you decide that $1 million will make you happy, but then when you get there you decide that $2 million is what you really want. We invest in money to make more money. We invest in purpose to make more purpose. We do not invest in money to make more purpose or vice versa. It just doesn't work that way.

And finally, you are doing it wrong if you think the act of making a lot of money today excuses you from pursuing purpose at the same time. We are really good at putting off those things that challenge us. While building a fiscal fortune isn't easy, it is eminently knowable. We know—or can learn fairly easily—how to save and invest, how to get a good job and earn a promotion. Investing and building businesses can be learned. Finding purpose, however, is a lot more difficult to define. This difficulty often tempts us to put off this important work until tomorrow. We wait until we have more time, more energy, more money. We wait until it's too late. Until we are lying on our deathbed, lamenting to our hospice doctor that we never did the things that were truly important to us. Don't let this be you!

After working with the dying for years and losing my father at a young age, I am intimately familiar with the concept that tomorrow is promised to no one. Our time on this Earth is limited and mostly uncontrollable. No one on their deathbed says that they wish they had made more money. No one regrets paying too little attention to their net worth.

They regret not pursuing those things that were important to them (purpose). They regret not finding people with similar interests (community). And they regret not strengthening the bonds with those who they cared most about (connections). In other words, they regret that they did not allow themselves to be happier.

WEALTH AND HAPPINESS
ARE NOT EXCLUSIVE

Up to this point, we have made this seem like a binary choice: either accumulate wealth or learn to build a sense of purpose and happiness. The truth, however, is a lot more hopeful. The key is to build enough material wealth to allow us to pursue our sense of purpose and happiness with greater ease. This often means that we have to be cognizant of our finances, learn how to invest, and pursue careers that also economically support us.

The good news is that this is very possible. Some will find jobs that fulfill their sense of purpose and thus enjoy the process of building wealth immensely. Others will sacrifice days, hours, or years to improve their financial situations with the intentional plan of creating more margin for purpose at a later date. And many will start with jobs they do not enjoy and incrementally mold them into a better fit. You might even start a side hustle or hobby business that eventually sustains you.

How you decide to create this purposeful life is totally up to you. But you have to be able to fund it.

The pot of gold at the end of the rainbow is happiness. While I have been very intentional in Part 1 of this book about defining *purpose* and the role little P purpose can play in happiness, Part 2 will be a deep dive into the power of meaning and how to bring your purpose to life through a process called **the climb**.

A PURPOSE PRESCRIPTION: PERFORMING A HOME AUDIT

- Clear your schedule for an hour on two separate occasions in the next week. If you can, turn off all electronics or silence your phone. Find a quiet room at home where you will not be disturbed. It's best to do this exercise when no one else is home.

- After spending a moment to relax and clear your mind of extraneous thoughts, stand up and walk through each room, nook, and cranny of your home. Open all the closets. Go into the basement if you have one. The idea is not to rush; but don't dilly-dally either. There is no need to focus on one object or room more than another. Just open yourself to being present.

- After ten minutes, return to the quiet space in which you started. Close your eyes and relax. Again, try to clear your mind for a moment. Push away the nagging thoughts that have been plaguing you all day.

- After taking a few deep breaths, think about the five most expensive things that you bought in the past that now inhabit the space you just walked through. Contemplate the joy you felt upon the purchase. How long did that joy last? Do you still get as great a thrill when your eye accidently catches that object now? There is no judgment here. The idea is to create awareness.

- After pondering your material possessions for a few more minutes, think about the five most important people in your life as reflected by what you saw when walking through your home. Maybe you had a picture of you and your mother standing in front of the Statue of Liberty from your last trip together. Possibly a book in your bookshelf given to you by a beloved mentor. Or maybe a piece of jewelry your long-time beau gave you for your anniversary.

- Consider how your feelings about those people have changed over the years. Have your love and passion grown or waned? Are those feelings static or ever-changing? How does this compare to thinking about your material possessions?

- Finally, move on to what makes you think of your life purpose and happiness (outside of other people). Is it the award on your office shelf for being the best programmer on your team? The collection of autographs displayed lovingly in your living room? The model airplane that took a full year to build and paint?

- Again, there are no right or wrong answers here. Meditate on what has felt purposeful in your life and whether your feelings surrounding those things have grown or changed. Do these things still make you feel warm and happy inside?

- After comparing and contrasting your feelings about these different categories, open your eyes and open up your phone or computer and go to your largest bank account. Imagine that I suddenly deposited $1 million into your account. How would it change your feelings about your material possessions, the people in your life, and your sense of purpose?

If you are not sure whether the extra money would make you happier, it is probably time to move on to Part 2 of this book, and better define the role of meaning in happiness and how to turn little P purpose into action. In Chapter 5, we will take the very first steps on what will become the climb!

PART 2: MEANING + PURPOSE = HAPPINESS

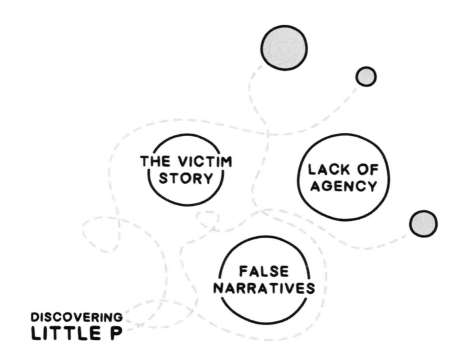

THE VICTIM STORY

LACK OF AGENCY

FALSE NARRATIVES

DISCOVERING
LITTLE P

"Happiness is the meaning and purpose of life, the whole aim and end of human existence."

—Aristotle

What is the true meaning of *happiness*—and is it a goal that we should truly strive for?

In Part 1 of this book, I have argued that there is a paradox when it comes to purpose. The type of purpose you choose to pursue could very well lead to anxiety and distress. When we shoot for big audacious goals that are easy to fail, we become a victim of big P Purpose. On the other hand, investing in activities that we enjoy the process of doing without an end goal in mind can lead to greater longevity, health, and happiness.

Ultimately, the choice is yours.

Yet understanding purpose doesn't necessarily mean that we will be happier people. The truth is that many of us have trouble even defining what the term *happiness* means. Certain individuals perceive joy as a fleeting biochemical occurrence, while others view it as the ultimate pursuit of humanity. Whether articulated as contentment, self-actualization, wellness, or—as suggested in my last book—purpose, identity, and connections, the essence endures. Our quest is unwaveringly for a robust sense of tranquility, inclusion, and the aspiration that our existence contributes meaning to a universe characterized by unpredictability. We are looking to build communities and foster better connections with the people we care about.

In Part 2 of *The Purpose Code*, I will completely redefine Aristotle's concept of happiness. While the ingredients are the same—meaning and purpose—we will turn them from abstract concepts into daily opportunities to take action.

While often used interchangeably, *meaning* refers to our cognitive understanding of the past, while *purpose* points us to action regarding our present and future. It turns out that we need both.

I will explore meaning in terms of the stories we tell ourselves about ourselves. Becoming the hero of our own journey makes the past bearable and the future limitless. But often, instead, we tell ourselves stories of victimization and helplessness.

Why do we do that?

And, finally, I will introduce the concept of **the climb**: a framework through which to understand how to take all we discovered about little P purpose in Part 1 and apply it to building a happier and healthier life today.

CHAPTER 5:
MEANING AND PURPOSE—TWO SIDES OF THE SAME COIN

Meaning and purpose form two sides of the happiness coin.

Meaning is focused on cognition and our ability to connect ideas and make sense of our past. It is more thought oriented and less action oriented. We tell ourselves stories about our lives that make it bearable—or, better yet, magical. Having a sense of meaning involves interpreting our past in such a way that we are the hero of our own adventure. It is not whether good or bad things happen to us, but how we interpret them and weave the tapestry of our lives.

Happy people tend to interpret the hardships of life as stepping stones that have somehow become a bridge to better and more successful times. Unhappy people see the past as uncontrollable and regard themselves as victims. This victim mentality projects to a future that is insecure and unstable—that is, unhappy.

> **Meaning** is a process focused on cognition and our ability to make sense of our past.

Purpose, however, is much more geared to action. Unlike meaning, purpose is present and future oriented. It's about both being in the moment and helping us project ourselves into the unknown.

To improve our sense of meaning, we need to come to terms with our past and draw connections between what seem like disparate events to feel a sense of connection and *meaningfulness*. When we struggle with such things, we can often find help through therapy and mental processing.

To improve our sense of purpose, we can engage in a process which I call *the climb*—the subject of the next chapter.

To better understand the difference between meaning and purpose, I want to introduce you to a brother and sister I met during a home visit on our hospice service. Although Carla was coming to the end of her prolonged battle with breast cancer, she still had stories to tell. Her twin brother, Miguel, sat patiently by her side tending to her every need.

Two siblings. Twins. A life lived together—yet one was abundantly happy, the other anything but.

TWIN PEAKS

During the life review I conducted with Carla one quiet morning, she retold the story of her life. It began with a miracle—and a tragedy. She and Miguel arrived in the world far too early. The midwife in her parents' inner-city neighborhood managed the delivery all by herself, miles from any doctors or hospitals. But while Carla and Miguel were born healthy against all the odds, their mother didn't survive the delivery.

This could have been the first among many tragedies (and in objective terms, it was); yet Carla never saw it that way. Instead, she dreamed about the ultimate sacrifice her mother made to help her and her twin come into the world. This sacrifice colored almost everything she did growing up. She felt special. Like the world had strained to breaking point just so she could survive and thrive.

Carla grew up with an odd sense of pride and belonging. Although there was never enough money, it never seemed to hinder her from doing what she wanted to do. Her father worked long hours and was almost never home, but this gave the twins space to develop into independent and capable kids. And when her father was home or had a day off, they had so much fun going to the local carnival or hanging out on the porch watching the world go by. They didn't live in the best of neighborhoods, but mostly avoided crime and theft. They really had nothing of value in their house to be stolen.

Carla's feelings of belonging and unconditional love from her mother's sacrifice led to a strong sense of self-love and confidence. The local school system was limited but didn't stop her from getting the education she needed and becoming the first of her family to go to college. There she met a man who treated her well and eventually became her husband.

Although he died way too young, they had a number of decades together in which they made their own family, with two sons and a daughter. Carla was an amazing mom. She showered her kids with the same love she imagined her own mother had for her: the unconditional love of a woman who had fought to bring her children into the world and died in the process.

Lying on her deathbed, Carla felt thankful for her twin brother, the husband who she hoped to see again after she passed, and her wonderful children who had grown up and made families of their own. The things in her house and bedroom that surrounded her in her last days were deeply meaningful and represented a life full of memories and joyous experiences.

Even in her last few days, Carla woke up every morning with the hope and expectation that something magical would happen. She believed that past was prelude. Whatever little bit of life was left over would be just as joyous and interesting as that which she had already lived.

She died at peace.

REVOLVING DOORS AND SHIFTING PERSPECTIVES

The day before Carla's death, I was privileged to sit down to talk to Miguel about his feelings regarding his twin sister's imminent passing. After we chatted for a while about his grief and his hopes for a peaceful death, I mentioned how Carla and I had rehashed some of their childhood struggles. What Miguel said next knocked me off my feet.

"Man, it was tough. I'm surprised we survived. Carla, though, always had it easier!"

He then spent the next half an hour telling me a completely different story about their childhood. After his mom died, his dad fell into a deep depression. Due to this, he got fired from almost every job he could find. They lived in poverty—often there was not enough food on the table to make their stomachs stop growling.

Part of the reason their mom had died was that they were too poor to afford routine medical care. The neighborhood they lived in was rough. They had to skip school on days when the threat of gang violence was so high they were afraid to leave the house. And when they did go to school, there were never enough books and the teachers themselves were defeated and disengaged.

Miguel had felt trapped. While Carla made extra money babysitting, he went to work for a local drug dealer. Although the money was good, he found himself in and out of jail for most of his teenage years.

When he did finally decide to straighten out, his spotted history made finding a legitimate job all but impossible. He had a number of relationship failures and ended up with a few kids with different women.

"How was I supposed to know how to be a parent with a dead mother and a father who had all but checked out?"

Miguel couldn't explain the difference in the lives that he and his twin sister had built. While they had almost the exact same genetics and environment growing up, Carla seemed to get all the breaks. She rolled with the punches effortlessly while he struggled on the ropes. Miguel wasn't exactly jealous of his sister, but the story he told himself about himself was that of a victim. He struggled with his love for a sister, who always seemed to have had it easier than he did.

"She was just lucky!"

MEANING AND STORY

To understand the difference between Miguel and Carla's perspectives is to understand the role meaning plays in happiness. Unlike purpose, meaning is very much focused on the past. It is the stories we tell ourselves about ourselves and the significance we attribute to those stories. The stories don't have to be accurate or true. In fact, it is often healthy to color our memory of the past with thoughts, emotions, and intentions. (This, as we have seen, can be done unhealthily too.)

When it comes to Carla and Miguel's recollections, was one more or less accurate than the other? Probably not. Most likely they would have agreed on the basic facts and timeline. The variation came in the interpretation. Carla chose to tell herself a story of triumph and overcoming. She recognized the difficult aspects of her life (having no mother, growing up poor, her father never being available) yet interpreted them as stepping stones instead of hindrances.

Have you ever found yourself doing the same? Can you think of a horrendous period in your life? Do you now think of yourself as a victim or a courageous hero who overcame the impossible?

Miguel saw himself as a victim. The story he told himself about his life was a tale of unfairness. He was born into a bad situation, never had the tools he needed to succeed, and was damned from the beginning. This was frustrating

The hero's journey is a literary device described by Joseph Campbell which follows a protagonist's journey of challenges, growth, and transformation.

to say the least. He saw the past as something uncontrollable. He had no agency. The meaning he ascribed to his life was one of loss, hurt, and unfairness.

Carla viewed herself much as the central figure in Joseph Campbell's **hero's journey.**[32]

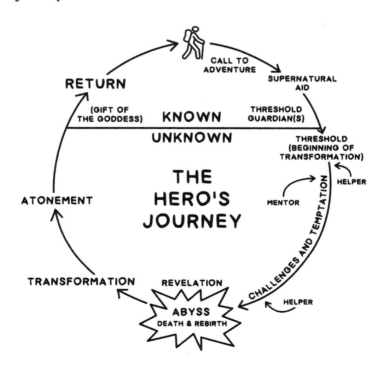

In the stories Carla told herself about herself, while venturing on the road of life, she often fell into the abyss. These experiences, however, transformed her and she climbed back out again stronger, more able, and more understanding. Because of this, even at the end of her life, Carla was basically happy and optimistic about what little future she had left. She had not only overcome hurdles in the past, but also thrived in unexpected ways. She was at peace.

Miguel's stories focused much more on victimhood. In what we can call the **victim's journey**, we are shaped by forces that are outside our control. We therefore look to the future with fear and trepidation. We have a very negative model of what the future will bring. For these reasons, Miguel shared none of Carla's sense of peace. In fact, he was downright unhappy.

MY HERO'S JOURNEY

I find myself identifying with Carla more than Miguel. I struggled with three main obstacles that had a profound impact on my life. My father died suddenly when I was seven. I had a learning disability that severely impacted my ability to read. And I was born a religious outsider in a fairly homogenous community and suffered through teasing and bullying for many years.

Were my trials and tribulations any worse than Carla's or Miguel's? After taking care of thousands of people throughout my medical career, I have realized that it probably doesn't matter. There is a moral equivalence in suffering. None of us escape unscathed. Each person's trauma radically impacts them because they have never experienced anything that could be considered worse or different.

Carla and I both suffered because of the deaths of our parents. Was hers worse than mine because it was her mother who died or because it happened at her birth? Who knows? I only experienced one of these situations, but its impact was just as meaningful to me as Carla's trauma was to her. We simply can't compare.

I would argue that the important aspect is not the individual severity of the trauma but the story we tell ourselves about it. My father's death was the spark that ignited my medical career despite a learning disability.

His death also was likely the reason that I eventually ended up in hospice medicine. There was no one to help me or my family in those last days when my father died. Now, I can fulfill that exact role.

How magical is that?

Burning out from medicine was not heartbreaking—it was nothing short of a miracle. It led to my study of personal finance and the discovery of the financial independence community. In this community, I have developed some of my most significant friendships as well as collaborative and creative relationships. Falling into the abyss of identity confusion became the nucleus of my book *Taking Stock*. While I might have struggled, I don't consider my journey a hardship. I recognize the beauty of the unexpected tosses and turns of life. I see growth. I see happiness.

Having a learning disability has taught me so much about life. Far from being a victim, I am blessed to have had this experience. In my time of greatest need, my mother was immediately there to provide answers and direction. My first-grade teacher was instrumental in advising us on how to get help and where to turn. My school system provided not one but two tutors and learning disability specialists. These specialists collaborated with my own outside tutor that we had hired, and they all developed a special, individualized curriculum to help me grow and learn.

I was so lucky.

I not only eventually learned how to read but became adept at something that would continue to serve me for the rest of my life: failure. I failed at school. I failed at sports. And as I got older, I even failed at romantic relationships. Yet, given the success of overcoming my learning disability, I saw failure as a natural building block to achieving better things. I decided that if failure was the worst thing that I would have to face, why not try to do really hard things? The story I told myself is that failure is not only natural and expected, but positive. That story, as with all the others that I am retelling, served me often as the years passed.

Being an outcast in my rather homogenous community was not easy when it came to religion. Although I had never invested in such things as a kid, the other children knew that I was different. And they teased me mercilessly. While this ended in fist fights for my older brother, for me it mostly meant isolation and abandonment. I remember a bunch of really tough years in elementary school.

However, this abandonment became the tablet on which I inscribed a new sense of self-reliance and direction. It was during this time that I developed my love of reading, working out, and many other self-directed activities that I still engage in today. My beliefs about equality and equity were also shaped during this period of my life. Being singled out and bullied based on my religion gave me new insights and empathy toward those who are different and often left out of society. I developed a social conscience that is obvious even today in my choice of guests and topics for my podcast.

These stories that I tell myself continuously evolve and change. With every new stage of life, I am looking back as well as forward. How do I reinterpret the past to not only understand but thrive in the present and future? **How do I remain the hero of my journey regardless of which way the path twists and turns?**

This habit of storytelling not only benefits people like Carla and me; it is super-important for all of us.

PERSONAL NARRATION AND MENTAL HEALTH

The benefits of ascribing meaning via storytelling have been well documented in scientific literature. The examples are overwhelming. Adler and fellow researchers explored the link between personal narrative and wellbeing.[33] They found increasing success in a four-step process:

- exploring personal narratives;
- reflecting on them;
- changing them; and
- sharing them.

While this process makes us more vulnerable, it also helps us learn and grow. It brings meaning to our struggles in the past and allows us to refine our conclusions in more positive terms.

As Pamela Rutledge says in her book *Exploring Positive Psychology:*

The Science of Happiness and Well-Being, "storytelling is everything."[34] Storytelling—or narrative—is fundamental to how we think and make meaning of the world. Whether we realize it or not, stories are at the center of everything we do. How we tell our stories controls our mood, our self-image, and our influence on others. Our stories can also dictate our future paths—and successes. Therefore, understanding storytelling not only is key to how we feel about ourselves and how we interact with others, but gives us valuable tools we can use to make change.

What has become increasingly clear is that we begin to feel better about ourselves as we tell stories of times when we were able to exert control over our lives, in particular our recoveries.[35] In fact, most forms of therapy or psychoanalysis are based on our ability to tell and retell our stories in such a way as to interpret traumatic events in better and more constructive ways.

There are myriad other benefits of becoming a master at narrative storytelling.[36] When we feel a connection to characters in a story (including ourselves), we get a surge of the neurohormone oxytocin, which is known to be related to a sense of empathy. In the case of our own stories, we build a deeper inner connection and *self*-empathy. Furthermore, studies show that the stories we tell about ourselves

Personal narrative is a form of storytelling told in the first person about one's own life and experiences.

can help build our successes and improve on failure. A study following adolescents showed that new personal narratives could have several positive effects on ongoing academic success.[37]

TRANSFORMING YOUR STORY

The good news is that it is very possible to transform your story and be more cognizant of the meaning you derive from the past. In fact, the field of **narrative therapy** helps people move past their problematic life stories and is key to overcoming roadblocks that may have previously held us back. By exploring this type of therapy, we may be able to recognize why

Carla and Miguel had such different interpretations of their childhood and circumstances. It might become clear why my father's death and my learning disability eventually became motivators of, instead of detractors from, my future accomplishments.

Narrative therapy is a form of therapy which aims to separate the individual from the problem.

The concept of narrative therapy was first introduced by Michael White and David Epston in the 1980s. The idea was to separate individual mistakes, difficult episodes, or life situations from the moralistic evaluation of the person themselves. In other words, *bad* things often happen to *good* people. Your personal value is not defined by your most difficult moments or mistakes.

There are several aspects to narrative therapy. The core tenets take a person through the following general steps:[38]

- understanding your story;
- deconstructing the dominant and often negative narratives;
- breaking these narratives into more manageable chunks;
- broadening your view and embracing healthier storylines;
- externalizing your story from your identity; and
- reauthoring the story to include more meaning and purpose.

These steps could be very beneficial for someone like Miguel. Writing down the story of his childhood would give him a better **understanding** of what exactly he went through. Next, he could **deconstruct** the negative narratives surrounding victimization and control. He might want to break down the narratives into smaller, more manageable chunks. That could begin with the death of his mother and progress to growing up poor or his involvement in selling drugs. As Miguel begins to reevaluate these narratives, he can begin the process of **broadening** his views of his childhood and realizing that the death of his mother and the poverty he endured were **external** realities and not part of a damaged identity. Finally, he can reauthor the story to include a much more heroic and self-empathizing version of his past.

Whether she thought about it specifically or not, this is exactly the path Carla took in rewriting the story of her own past. As in the Aristotle quote at the beginning of this section, *happiness is the meaning and purpose of life*. Carla created meaning by telling and retelling the stories of her life in ways that made it feel magical and created a hero in the image of her past self. But, as the quote also says, meaning is only half the equation— one side of the coin. True happiness also requires purpose.

And when I am talking about purpose, of course, I am talking of the kind that is life affirming and lengthening, not the kind that is anxiety ridden. I am talking of little P purpose.

HEADS I WIN, TAILS YOU LOSE

As we said at the beginning of this chapter, meaning and purpose are the two sides of the happiness coin. While for the most part, up until now we have focused on the concept of meaning and how it relates to our ultimate goals, we will briefly return to purpose here before diving into the deep end in the next chapter. It is time to pivot away from discussing the different types of purpose (from now on, assume we are talking exclusively about little P purpose) and toward why it is so important when it comes to happiness.

Meaning, as we have discussed, is focused on our past. We are reimagining both our good and bad memories, our triumphs and traumas, with a very specific purpose in mind: to create a better future and present. While meaning focuses on the past, the boon at the end of struggling with it is to focus on *today*. Focusing on today (and tomorrow) is all about purpose. It is how we project ourselves into the future. Because of this, purpose in general is action oriented. We are moving out of the realm of thought and toward those activities that we want to be engaged in now.

Meaning must come before purpose. They must be sequential. Miguel will find it hard to discover little P purpose in his life until he starts the practice of narrative storytelling. Like Clara, he must deconstruct the hurts and traumas of his childhood to rewrite a new narrative in which he feels like he not only survived but became the hero of his own story. Only then will he be ready to begin working on today.

Like Miguel, once we move past the victimhood mindset, the present and future become limitless. We need this limitlessness as a backdrop for exploring a framework that can help better build purpose into our lives. Just knowing how to create purpose is not enough: we must then use that purpose to create happiness. The way we do this is the topic of the next chapter.

It is called **the climb,** and it is the key to mastering the second half of the happiness equation.

A PURPOSE PRESCRIPTION: PERSONAL NARRATIVE AUDIT

- Clear your schedule for an hour on two separate occasions in the next week. If you can, turn off all electronics or silence your phone. Find a quiet room where you will not be disturbed. It is best to do this exercise when no one else is home.

- After spending a moment to relax and clear your mind of extraneous thoughts, think about two or three of the most traumatic events in your past. It's okay if this doesn't feel good when you start. Take long, deep breaths if you feel yourself getting anxious or triggered.

- For each traumatic event, spend a few minutes thinking about if you are at peace with the memory. Does it still bother you? Was it a learning experience? Positive or negative? How does this trauma creep into your everyday life?

- Now discard any of the traumatic events that feel comfortable, resolved, or have a silver lining associated with them.

- For those traumatic events that still feel uncomfortable, undertake the following exercise:

  1. Understand your trauma: Think back to the specific details. What exactly happened? Why did it happen? Who were the parties involved? Remember the trauma can be a one-time event or an ongoing issue like growing up in poverty. The duration of the trauma is unimportant.

  2. Deconstruct the different stories you tell yourself about this trauma: are there multiple stories? Are there multiple different components or themes? Feelings of helplessness, abandonment, or physical pain?

  3. Break down the narrative into more manageable parts: Separate these different components and contemplate them one at a time.

  4. Broaden your view: Are there more positive and healthier storylines that you can attach to the unchangeable realities of the trauma? Can you come to terms with the idea that you did the best you could in the circumstances— that there were forces either out of your control or that you weren't capable of managing at that age or in that mental state?

  5. Externalize the story from your identity. Although the trauma happened to you, the story is not in fact you. Realize that even if you are not proud of how you conducted yourself, bad decisions do not make you a bad person. We are all entitled to have good days and horrible days without either of them defining us.

  6. Now for the fun part. Reauthor your story in a way that brings you a new sense of meaning and maybe even leads

to purpose in your future. How can you learn to see this traumatic event in a more positive light? Your current self is a product of all that has happened to you, both good and bad. How can you feel proud of who you have become?

- After completing the above steps, I suggest you do no further work on these issues for at least a week or two. Let your thoughts fade in and out of your mind without the pressure of trying to resolve anything. If you are feeling distress, it may be a good time to discuss things with your loved ones or therapist. While working on our past sense of meaning is hard, it is key to building a framework of purpose in our current life.

Take a deep breath, do a few warm-up stretches and take a few breaths. It's time to take on the climb. Which, of course, is the topic of the next chapter …

CHAPTER 6:
THE CLIMB

In the last chapter, we classified the two key components of happiness as *meaning* and *purpose*. While meaning mainly exists in the realm of cognition, purpose relates to present-day activities. Our actions are embodiments of purpose. Thus, in order to help you build the life you want to live, I have created a framework in which to evaluate and create fulfillment—to turn purpose into action.

I call this framework *the climb*.

In this chapter, we will return to Sarah, our fashion journalist, who after doing her purpose exercises has been reacquainted with her love of horses. Although Sarah now has an anchor—a stable place to begin building a happier life by pursuing purpose—she still has many questions about how to transform her life with her newfound knowledge.

The climb is a framework for building a life of little P purpose.

"Do I have to quit my job?"

"How do I turn my passion into a life I love?"

"What if I fail?"

"What if I change my mind?"

"Could I destroy my current life and then decide I was wrong?"

Sarah's reaction, and her plethora of questions, are completely understandable. Although we may just be starting to take notice of our own internal whisperings urging us to a more gratifying way of living, it doesn't make taking action any easier. The climb will provide a template to help Sarah—and you—transition smoothly while minimizing fear and providing guidance.

Change is difficult. Overcoming this challenge will require not only courage but an enhanced awareness of time and time management. While many mistakenly believe that time is a changeable entity or commodity, it is neither. By understanding this fundamental truth, we learn how to work within this framework. We realize that time waits for no one. Sarah has every reason in the world to put off making such a dramatic transformation, except for the most important one.

Whether we want to admit it or not, our days are numbered. And there is nothing, absolutely nothing, that we can do about it. If we don't begin engaging in the climb today, there will be less time to do so tomorrow.

The climb depends mainly on two aspects: first, filling our time with activities that are joyful or important to us; and second, leaving room for incremental gain.

The activities we find joyful are particular to who we are as people. It could be a fascination with horses, selling baseball cards, or working in a soup kitchen or homeless shelter. The details are not nearly as important as being engaged in activities where we enjoy the process regardless of the outcome. This is fundamental to the idea of the purpose paradox, which we introduced in Chapter 2.

In this chapter, we will examine how we define a climb, how we incorporate different climbs into our lives, and when it is time to get off one mountain and search for a new one. In doing so, I will show how I built a few specific climbs into my life, like podcasting and writing; and I will make some suggestions on how Sarah can take her newfound purpose anchor and do the same.

TIME WAITS FOR NO ONE

In my last book, *Taking Stock*, I made the argument that time is not a commodity. You cannot buy or sell it, spend it, waste it, wait for it or let it catch up to you. Time simply passes, no matter how we try to manipulate it. We cannot pause the days and years. They simply march on.

We do, however, have some control over the activities we are involved in as time passes. I like to think of each human being as having a certain number of time slots. These could be hours, days, weeks, or years. We have no clue how many of these times slots we have. We should be mindful of our own mortality. My father died at the age of 40. In my hospice program, I have taken care of people in their 20s and those over 100 years old on the same day.

So, what are we to do? The answer, I believe, is to fill as many of these time slots with things we love and remove as many loathsome activities from these same coveted allocations as possible. In order to perform this task, we must be clear and intentional about that which is important to us. We must continuously ask the question: "Does this activity warrant my time and attention?"

There are two tools which can help us with these determinations. As mentioned previously, the art of subtraction allows us to scratch out that which is no longer serving us. But without the joy of addition, we find ourselves facing an empty canvas with no meaningful brushstrokes to fill the void. We colloquially call this "wasting time" when we are discussing our day—or "wasting space" when we are discussing art.

It is in the **joy of addition** that we take our first steps toward the base of the climb—toward painting our masterpiece. By adding in purposeful activities one at a time, we are incrementally improving our quality of life. We are tipping the scales in favor of joy and away from obligation. By engaging in these activities, we feel happiness regardless of whether the end product is pleasing. There is no luck involved here. This is the essence of being in the moment.

Sarah now has some difficult decisions to make. Which activities will she subtract from her life, and which climbs will she build in? While we cannot answer these questions for her, we can provide some guidance. This is a particularly good time for Sarah to evaluate her finances. Is she beholden to her job? Does that job provide any attachment to her purpose anchors? If Sarah were to leave her job, could she find another which felt more purposeful and still paid the bills?

Sarah is standing at the base of the mountain with her hiking shoes on. It's time she learned to take her first steps.

THE CLIMB

The climb is how we turn the concept of purpose into action. After performing the exercises in Chapter 3, many (like Sarah) will feel that they have a better idea of what little P purpose looks like in their lives. They may have two or three ideas or anchors that feel important. The climb is the process through which we take the grounding these anchors provide and turn it into a base camp or starting point for meaningful activities.

The nature of these activities is completely up to you. For Roman, his anchor of baseball turned into a business in which he sold baseball cards to local schoolkids. For me, the anchor of writing turned into a blog— originally about medicine, but eventually about personal finance. Sarah, as we have discussed, loves horses. Every person can have a different anchor, and one person can have many anchors. The key is to identify those themes that light you up and then build climbs around them.

Purpose anchors are themes around which we can start to create our climbs. These themes are based on little P Purpose.

How do we do this?

Simple: we engage in activities that incorporate these anchors, but do so in a very specific way. There are rules on how to participate in a healthy climb. These rules will remind you of the properties that define little P purpose. First, your climb should never be goal oriented—it should be goal agnostic. If all you can concentrate on is the top of the mountain, you are bound to falter. Goals are like the peaks after a valley. While in the valley, all you can see is the nearest peak. However, after making your way out, you realize that the top of the mountain is even further off. There is not just one but a series of peaks. It is far better to participate only in climbs in which you actually enjoy the terrain—the process.

We can be very clear here. Sarah should avoid climbs with ultra-specific goals. At least in the beginning, she should not rely on her love of horses to make a living. The goal of making money may turn the activity that she is very fundamentally motivated to do into a chore. Studies of behavioral theory show that financial incentives often turn joyful activities into loathsome ones.

Sarah should also probably avoid dreams of fame or unrealistic achievements. She most likely will not become an Instagram influencer when it comes to equestrian sports; nor will she ride in the Olympics. By adopting such dreams, she would not only inevitably experience failure, but also be coopting someone else's version of purpose. It would not be serving her needs.

Second, your climb must be made of activities that bring you joy in the doing. The climb is 100% process oriented. There is no reality other than the joy of each step. There is no past or future; the climb is present oriented. The aftermath cannot change that which has already passed. While new opportunities and accolades are never frowned upon, the worth of an activity is not measured by that which comes later.

To begin her climb, Sarah should search out activities and communities surrounding her joy of horse riding. She should recognize that some of these activities will fit like a glove, while others will be too small or too large. The litmus test, for Sarah, will be to be cognizant, at the end of the day, of whether she feels that her time was well spent.

Third, you should not be able to fail your climb. Don't be fooled by the F word; failure is just another reference to goal-seeking, and we're not doing that here. Success equals showing up and doing the thing that is important to you. This is absolutely critical. The minute we begin to assign qualitative or quantitative values to our efforts is the minute we start searching again for the peak. If your "goal" is to enjoy the process, there is no endpoint defining victory or success. Success is starting up the mountain.

Fourth, it is reasonable to incorporate an aspect of incremental gain into your climb. Unlike a larger goal or destination, "incremental gain" means finding controllable ways to feel like you are making progress. This might mean reading around the subject, attending a class, or having a mentor teach you new ways to improve the climb. The goal of improvement, again, is greater enjoyment or pleasure in your skill set. The goal is not to reach a higher peak or travel to another destination.

Sarah should expect that as she gets more involved in her climb, she will be able to set personal plans for learning and improvement. This might include learning how to ride side-saddle or maybe spending an afternoon a week working on showjumping. She should enjoy the prospect of getting better or broadening her skills.

Finally, we do not have to be monogamous when it comes to the climb. We can have multiple climbs. Some may be more important than others. A climb may last for a lifetime or be limited to a single season of our lives. Sarah may find that, while working at the stable, she volunteers with a local group of Down's syndrome kids who want to learn how to ride. Her love of the children and deeper understanding of their situation may lead her to volunteer with a local advocacy group to increase awareness. The climb may ignite a passion that lasts for years; or she may move on to another climb in a few months. There is no right or wrong.

The Five Commandments (the Rules of the Climb)

- Your climb should never be goal oriented.
- Being on your climb must bring you joy.
- You cannot fail your climb.
- Climbs can incorporate incremental gain.
- Monogamy is optional when it comes to purpose.

RECOMMENDATIONS FOR SARAH

Our recommendations for Sarah thus become rather evident. The easiest way to start is by practicing the joy of addition. She can take a few hours on the weekend, when she is doing something unimportant, and replace that activity with the beginning of a climb. This could be volunteering at the local stable or perhaps starting a blog about her love of horses.

Over the weeks that follow, she can evaluate her newfound activities. Are they joyful? Do they feel important when she is doing them, regardless of what happens afterwards? Is this a better use of her time than whatever activities she was doing before? These activities may provide other opportunities to learn and grow. Maybe she could get a part-time job at the stable, which not only would be a good use of her time but might also create some financial breathing room in her life.

As Sarah embraces these new activities, she should take a long, hard look at her work environment. Does it contain elements of this climb or other climbs for her? If not, are there some aspects of work she finds appealing? Maybe she could spend more time at her current job doing enjoyable tasks such as editing creative writing. Although this may not be the climb related to her anchor involving her love of horses, it is still a climb.

Whether Sarah decides to change jobs or not is completely up to her. She may stay in her job as a fashion editor because it pays well enough to support the climbs she is creating in other parts of her life. Or she may decide that her time would be better filled by finding a job at a magazine that incorporates her climbs. She could look for a magazine that focuses on horses or horse-related sports.

Sarah should remain open to other opportunities and climbs that fill her life with purpose. She may find other passions that consume her. Her love of music or interest in developing her skills in storytelling may become new anchors. These anchors can then lead her in new directions. It may even be that after a few years, Sarah decides that she no longer enjoys her time at the stable on the weekends. It behooves her then to replace that activity with one that is more consistent with her current interests. There is no guilt in substituting one climb for another. The goal is to continuously replace mediocrity with joy.

Although the initial goal of the climb is not the formation of relationships, building a community and making connections will come naturally. Sarah will find herself being intentional and authentic around others who share her interests and passions. This will provide ample opportunity to connect with those who wander in and out of her sphere. In fact, she may find that while horse riding is slightly less thrilling than before, the group of girlfriends that she meets every Friday at the stable to ride with and have dinner with afterwards is reason enough to continue.

GOAL AGNOSTIC BUT
NOT GOAL PHOBIC

As mentioned in previous chapters, I have been very clear about the toxicity of goals. They can create a sense that only once an endpoint is achieved can a person be happy. We want Sarah to thrive regardless of whether she meets some specified endpoint. One should never base a climb on a goal—especially not a goal that has been taken from someone else's life or Instagram account.

This does not mean that all goals are bad or that we shouldn't have them. Our climbs should be goal agnostic, not goal phobic. In other words, Sarah may develop a number of goals along the way. She may decide that she would like to eventually earn a living by writing freelance for equestrian periodicals. This may be her big audacious goal. She loves to write and she has a passion for the subject of horses. Thus, Sarah has created a goal *within* her climb; but there is an important difference here. No matter the outcome, she is still being a good steward of her time. She may succeed or she may not. She may only cover half her income and transition to working part-time at the fashion magazine. By doing this, she can replace activities that she doesn't like with ones that are part of her climb.

She wins even when she loses (fails).

The size of the goal doesn't matter. It can be big and unachievable or small and simple. The only requirement is that the success or failure has no effect on the climb. No matter what happens, Sarah will still pursue a life of purpose. She will continue to use the joy of addition to build into her daily life as many of these climbs as possible and use the art of subtraction to rid herself of activities that no longer fulfill her.

Even better, she can incorporate the idea of incremental gain into these goals. She can use her freelance skills to replace small increments of her income to slowly free herself of more burdensome money-making activities. She might never cover her income 100%, but each step forward will feel like its own tiny victory.

CLIMBS GONE BAD

There is no rule that says that we have to hold on to a specific climb for the rest of our lives. Although the techniques we discussed in Chapter 3 often point us in the direction of lifelong interests and values, sometimes we change. We have different seasons in our life punctuated by new responsibilities and new interests. There is no reason why we shouldn't embrace this.

There are several signs that a climb is no longer serving you. If you encounter any of these, it is time to re-evaluate if this climb is still a good use of your time. Remember, the goal is to fill as much of your time as is prudent with purposeful activities. It is quite possible that activities that used to be purposeful will no longer feel so. Let's discuss some things that should trigger you to question whether you want to continue on a given climb.

The first is that you find you are regretful of time spent on a particular climb because you would rather be doing something else. Sarah, for instance, may find that her love of freelance writing has become even more pronounced. Now, she wishes she had her Saturday mornings open to write. She is most productive upon waking, curling up with a warm cup of coffee and an empty computer screen. But there is a problem: her riding lessons are at the same exact time. She could move her lessons to Sunday, but that is when she goes to church with her mom and stepfather. It's not that Sarah has lost her love of riding; it's just that she has other more exciting or nurturing activities to fill these time slots.

Maybe she should cancel the lessons?

Another obvious sign is when a climb becomes too goal oriented, and happiness depends on attaining that goal. When Sarah starts to compete at race jumping, she finds it to be fun and exhilarating. But say it turns out that the team at her stable is ultra-competitive. Sarah finds herself happy on practice or competition days only if she performs well. On days of poor performance, she returns home sullen and wonders why she competed in the first place. She now feels good only based on the outcome, and not on the one thing she can control: showing up and being involved in the process. A change is clearly needed.

It may also be time to depart from a climb due to factors that have nothing to do with you yourself, or even the activity. A major part of the joy, for Sarah, of riding on Friday afternoons might be the group of friends who accompany her and go out for the evening afterwards. Unfortunately, one of those friends moves away and another has an accident and can no longer ride. Sometimes when you take away the community and connections around a climb, the climb loses something irreplaceable. Instead, Sarah makes plans with her friends to go out on another night and skip the stable altogether.

Finally, as much as you may like a given activity or subject, you may realize that pursuing this climb has not led to building a community and better connections. This may be fine for some people. There are many out there who are loners and who can completely enjoy life without other people attached. While this could be you, most of us want the pot of gold at the end of the rainbow. That pot of gold, when it comes to the climb, is the community you connect with through these joyous activities.

If your climb is not connecting you with other people, it might be a sign that it is time to move on.

DON'T JUST TAKE MY WORD FOR IT

Don't just take my word for it. A number of scientific studies have examined the relationship between meaningful activities and happiness. Hooker and colleagues examined how engaging in meaningful activities is essential to meaning, salience, and psychological wellbeing.[39] The study, which involved 160 participants, consisted of a self-monitoring group who answered questions regarding physical activity, mood, and meaning salience (i.e. the frequency of thinking about purpose and meaning). The results showed that engaging in meaningful activities was associated with a more positive mood, life satisfaction, purpose in life, and vitality.

Another group of studies focused on loneliness during the COVID-19 pandemic. One specifically recruited international university students in Taiwan. Researchers used the word *flow* to describe the state of being totally engaged or engrossed in what you are doing. They found that flow, while engaging in enjoyable activities that require concentration and skill, significantly reduced loneliness.[40]

Finally, a 2022 study in the *Journal of Applied Gerontology* looked at how engagement in favorite activities affected the cognition, mental health, and functional ability of geriatric adults.[41] They found that in cognitively healthy people, engagement in favorite activities was associated with greater functional independence, decreased depression and anxiety, and better performance on memory measures.

The science is clear: those who engage in climbs are happier. Period.

I AM CURRENTLY ON SEVERAL CLIMBS

I don't need scientific evidence to prove to me the importance of climbs and how they can lead to happiness. I have lived it. My journey started when I realized that the main climb I had been pursuing my whole life—being a doctor—was no longer serving me. All of the signs were there. I dreaded waking up to go to work in the morning. There were so many other things I wanted to do with my time, including writing and eventually podcasting.

Podcasting, for me, is a great example of a climb. It is part of my purpose because there is no better feeling, for me, than sitting behind a microphone and having engaging conversations. I would do this even if no one listened. Even if I had zero downloads per year. Yet becoming a better interviewer, finding more interesting guests, and improving my sound quality are all small steps that make this climb even more appealing.

I am making my way further up the mountain.

This does not mean that I enjoy absolutely every moment I spend working on my podcast. There are some mornings when I wake up and feel uninspired to conduct yet another interview. Other days, the idea of editing even one more minute of audio makes me want to crawl into my bed and hide. The difference, however, compared to those difficult days of burnout as a physician is that this is a climb that I exercise complete control over. I can head back down the mountain at any time I choose and look toward other peaks and valleys.

I am answerable only to myself and, more broadly, my community of listeners. There is no boss telling me what I can or can't do. No outside force exerting itself on my daily schedule.

Podcasting and writing, however, weren't enough. There was still much room to build other climbs. One was exercise. I had hated working out at times in my life, but now I focused only on those activities that I like. I often walked instead of running and played sports instead of lifting weights. I also reinvigorated my love of reading. Not reading that was focused or goal driven, but frivolous, joyful reading. I checked out almost every sci-fi or fantasy book I could find, and spent countless hours in a lawn chair inhaling my favorite types of stories.

We started this chapter by discussing how happiness is basically made up of meaning and purpose. The way we pursue purpose out in the world is by creating these meaningful climbs to help engage our time. By giving recommendations for Sarah as well as describing my own climbs, I am providing you with the framework to start building happiness into your life.

A good part of that happiness is to realize that time is both finite and cannot be commoditized. It passes no matter what we do. Thus, we need to create as much happiness in however much time we have on this Earth. We do this through the art of subtraction and the joy of addition. We subtract out that which is not working in our lives and add in as much time devoted to climbs as possible.

This is what the research supports, and this is what I did in my own life. The benefit is that I am happier, more content, and more engaged than at any other time in my life. My schedule is completely under my control and full of activities that I like to do.

Most importantly, these activities have connected me to a community of people that create even more meaning for me. The virtuous cycle continues. My happiness has made me a better father and husband. I am also a better friend. Which, of course, reminds me of one important warning. You might think that your sense of purpose revolves around your loved ones, or that your climb should be family. While this sounds enticing, I think it is completely the wrong way to build a life of purpose.

Want to know why? We will address this question in Chapter 8; but first, I want to take a detour into the world of privilege. What if you don't have enough money to buy climbing shoes? We'll tackle this tough question after a quick exercise.

A PURPOSE PRESCRIPTION: PERFORMING A TIME AUDIT

- Clear your schedule for an hour on two separate occasions in the next week. If you can, turn off all electronics or silence your phone. Find a quiet place where you will not be disturbed.

- Restart your phone and open the calculator app. Multiply 7 x 24. This is the number of hours in every week. Subtract 56 hours (8 x 7) to account for sleeping. Now subtract 16 hours (2 x 7) for grooming and 21 hours (3 x 7) for eating. This should leave you with 75 hours.

- Put the phone away. I don't want you to look at any kind of calendar or organizer. This is purely a mental exercise.

- How many of those 75 hours are you currently using to be involved in some climb or another? It might be easier to mentally break them down into a few different categories—maybe work related, lifestyle maintenance (e.g., kids, home), and leisure.

- Start with your work allocation. Let's assume you work eight hours a day and five days a week. How many of those 40

---

hours could be considered part of a climb? Is there anything you love about work? Any passions? Any activities that you would do even if you weren't being paid?

- Look at those activities involved in lifestyle maintenance and leisure. What do you do around the house? What do you do in your free time? How fulfilling are those tasks?

- After you are finished, try to calculate what percentage of that 75 hours is spent pursuing climbs and what percentage is used up on things that you either do not like or are required to do.

- How lopsided are the percentages? Do you spend 10% of the time on climbs? 70%? There is no right answer here. In fact, those who spend the lowest percentage of their time on climbs have the most room for improvement. Give yourself the grace of acceptance regardless of where you fall on the spectrum.

- Were there lots of blank spaces where you weren't engaged in anything good or bad? Does that bother you?

- In this chapter, we discussed the art of subtraction and the joy of addition. What could you add or subtract from your schedule to improve your numbers? Remember that every time you create a meaningful activity or dispose of an indifferent one, you are improving your percentages.

CHAPTER 7:
WHAT IF YOU CAN'T AFFORD CLIMBING SHOES?

Naysayers will argue that pursuing purpose or engaging in the climb is a privilege that mostly belongs to the well-off. They will point out that the art of subtraction or the joy of addition assumes a certain amount of margin in life—margin that is available only to those who were born with money, have a high-paying job, or encounter some other form of good fortune. Your average person is just working their tail off to make an *honest* living.

While I have received this criticism from many different corners, the vehemence is greatest among the young. Andy, a neighbor who had stumbled upon my first book, said it best: "I don't have *time* to worry about purpose. At the end of the day, I am so wrecked all I want to do is watch a little Netflix and go to sleep."

Struggling to make ends meet with a liberal arts education and a lack of high-paying jobs, he was working at a local nonprofit that could barely afford to pay him enough to cover his monthly rent. The idea that he could invest his time or energy in building a better life seemed far-fetched. Andy was at the beginning of his career yet felt beaten. He not only had no idea how to begin one of these climbs; he had zero margin in his life to search for one.

How do you start the climb if you can't afford a good pair of climbing shoes?

In this chapter, we will address the concerns of Andy and many others who feel they can't afford the climb. Whether it be money, energy, or time, the cost of such pursuits appears to be too high. Is that really the case—or are there things we can do about it?

MONEY IS A TOOL, NOT A GOAL

When I met Andy, he was living down the street, renting a unit in a duplex. He preferred Evanston because of its proximity to the city, his nonprofit job, and his parents, who lived nearby in the house where he grew up. He had graduated college the year before and had struggled to find a job related to his major. He was hoping to secure a position in marketing or advertising, but a nasty turn in the local job market left him with many bills but little income.

He didn't like working for his current employer. His daily activities were at best boring, at worst painful. He was expected to work longer than usual hours for very little pay. That pay, however, was better than he could get at a local restaurant and looked more impressive on his résumé. He usually spent most of the day on his feet and often was exhausted when he left the office at quitting time.

When he first began working, he spent his nights and weekends looking for a better, higher-paying job, but his efforts bore no fruit. He found himself frustrated and worn out—not just physically but mentally. He had discovered my first book, *Taking Stock*, online and ordered it when he recognized that I was a neighbor. You can imagine my surprise when he approached me on the street one day.

Andy was despondent. He so badly wanted to build a life of purpose, identity, and connections, yet felt that it was an impossible task. How could he subtract parts of his workday when that job was necessary to fund his basic lifestyle? How could he start adding purposeful activities when he had no money or energy at the end of each day?

Andy felt like he was trapped by his need to make money. His current job was his sole source of income and, while far from ideal, was the only reasonable role he could find. Andy felt stuck, in much the same way as I imagine many of you are feeling as you read these words. Are you hanging on to a job because you have to? Are you putting off creating a sense of purpose or starting the climb because you are strapped for cash or time—or both?

The mistake here is forgetting that money is a tool, not a goal.

Why is this such a mistake?

MONEY IS MARGIN

Money is a horrible goal, for so many reasons. Mostly because, at its most basic, money is potential energy. It has no value except what it can accomplish. Money itself never made anyone happy. It is the use of money that, when done correctly, can create meaning and purpose in our lives. And meaning and purpose can eventually turn into happiness.

When we make money a goal, we often find ourselves unhappy upon reaching the top of the mountain. Because money is a mirage or false destination, getting there feels hollow. *Now what?* The answer, usually, is to make more money. How is this fulfilling?

The other extreme is to be overwhelmed with fear that we will lose what we have gained. Loss aversion makes us more scared of losing money than we ever were of not making it in the first place.

In Andy's case, money became an all-or-nothing equation. He either had enough money and could start to build these climbs into his life now, or he didn't and was doomed to endure a horrible existence. Since he clearly didn't have enough money at the time I met him, he had a rather depressing outlook on the future. He became focused on the belief that without more money, he would never have enough margin to create freedom.

I cannot argue with Andy's basic premise. He is right. Money is margin. It is a tool that helps us exchange one type of potential energy for another. If I have money, I can pay for someone to clean my house or cut my grass. This allows me to fill my time with other activities—activities I may find more purpose oriented. Because Andy didn't have enough of this tool, he felt that all was lost.

What I'd like to convince you of in this chapter is that while money is a great tool, a great creator of margin, it is only one of many. Given Andy does not have much of this tool—or the likelihood of generating more soon—he must reach for other tools in his toolbelt. My biggest challenge was showing Andy that he actually had a full toolbelt already.

Perhaps you do too, without knowing it.

WHAT'S IN YOUR TOOLBELT?

Once you recognize that money is only one of many tools, you realize how many versions of "capital" you have. Andy, for instance, is 22 years old. As a 22-year-old, he has far more energy and fewer aches and pains than I do at 50. He can sleep less and work longer. He also has fewer responsibilities weighing him down. He doesn't have a spouse or kids. He doesn't have a mortgage. Andy can pick up and leave the country tomorrow; there is little to stop him.

His family and relationships are also important tools in his toolbelt. As we will suggest in the next section, Andy can utilize some of these connections to improve his situation. One of the most potent forms of capital is **human capital**. When we tap our friends and family as resources, we get access to all their knowledge, abilities, and relationships. There is a common saying for pilgrims walking the historic *Camino de Santiago* (the ancient pilgrimage trails to the shrine of St James the Apostle in northwestern Spain). They say that when you are down and destitute on your pilgrimage, "*the Camino will provide.*"

Well, *people* are your *Camino*. Those who have strong connections find that the universe takes care of them in the form of helping hands.

Your passions and knowledge are also often untapped tools that can provide in surprising ways. Roman found that his passion for baseball cards, and his first employee Ryan's knowledge of the market, turned his floundering antiques business into a rousing success. Knowledge and passion often cost very little money, but they can certainly create wealth.

And finally, in addition to friends and family, the larger communities that you belong to can also become levers to success and help create the kind of life you want to live. Communities come in all shapes and sizes. Maybe it is the church you belong to, or the university you graduated from, or being a foreigner abroad among other foreigners. You probably belong to many more communities than you are aware of. Those communities define you and can help when you are in need.

HOW ANDY CAN GET HIS
GROOVE BACK

Realizing that, while he may lack the tool of extra money, he has other tools to work with, Andy can rethink his ability to begin the climb. He may not have climbing shoes—but maybe he can make headway with a good walking stick and an ample supply of water. What resources does Andy have available to him? What resources do you?

Andy, as said, most definitely has the advantages of youth and time. Lacking the responsibilities of family and home ownership, most of his time outside of work is unspoken for. Working 8:00 am to 6:00 pm every day is exhausting, but the likelihood is that a 22-year-old will have some energy left over on the weekend. A simple solution is for Andy to start a passion-driven side hustle for a few hours every Sunday afternoon.

This side hustle should have a few basic characteristics. First, it should be connected to some type of purpose anchor. For instance, Andy was a serious competitive bike rider and raced throughout high school. He loves bikes and learned how to fix almost any mechanical problem after maintaining his racing bike by himself for the many years that he competed.

Although that was a long time ago, Andy is still very much part of the bike-racing community. He still knows a few of the people who work for the national association and set up local races. Using the tool of his free time on Sundays, and the tools of passion and community in the racing world, could Andy not make a few extra bucks (doing something he loves) by fixing other people's damaged bikes? He already has the tool of knowledge that came from trial and error as a high-school student working on his own wheels. What does he have to lose?

Let's jump six months into the future. There are a few different possibilities. If Andy finds success and builds a little side hustle that generates a few extra dollars, he might rejoice in the fact that he has created enough margin to cut his hours at work. What if he could work four days a week instead of five? If so, Andy has not only brought purpose into his life but also embarked on his first climb. Even more importantly, he has subtracted out a full nine hours a week of work that he loathes and replaced it with three hours a week of purposeful activities.

This is winning!

Maybe Andy is willing to work seven or even eight hours on Sunday. This might generate enough business to hire a local high-school kid and teach them to help out around the garage. With expanded hours and extra help, could Andy eventually leave his job or go down to half-time? And if the bike-fixing business is no longer fulfilling—or becomes more bothersome than his job—can he not just quit and return?

There is another outcome, of course, that we must also explore. What if Andy dutifully works over the next six months on Sundays and can never build a significant book of business? He goes to the racetrack and fixes one or two bikes, but at most covers a few expenses and maybe an extra night of eating out a week. But, regardless, he enjoys being back at the track and seeing old friends and coaching young kids.

This situation is just as good. True, Andy hasn't created any economic margin. He also hasn't subtracted any hours from his horrible job. Yet now he is spending three or four hours every week doing something full of joy and purpose, even if it doesn't make any money. For better or worse, Andy has started the first steps of a climb anchored to his love of bikes. He may switch things around and try to earn money as a racing coach; or he might be happy to continue his little business and be content with the fun of pursuing a new hobby.

Either way, Andy is now firmly embarked on the climb.

We haven't even begun to explore the other tools in his toolbelt. Andy's parents live just a few miles away from him. Could he convince them to let him move back into his family home at reduced rent (or none at all)? If so, Andy may find that he has again created margin through his relationships. The extra money he pockets could go to subtracting work hours or to adding in purposeful activities that cost money.

I haven't yet mentioned that "Andy" is short for "Andre." His name was Americanized when his family moved from Portugal to the United States when he was seven years old. Ever since, he has been fascinated by his home country. His family comes from the city of Porto, and throughout his childhood they visited almost yearly. Because of his inquisitive nature, Andy explored just about every nook and cranny of his childhood town. He devoured every historical article and book he could find. It was a passion. One day he wanted to return to Porto to live and bring up a family.

Why not now? Andy could take part in a practice called **geoarbitrage**. He could move back to Porto and live for a fraction of the cost of living in the United States. There is an American company that pays young people to give tours in English in foreign cities. Maybe he could work for this company and be paid like an American, but live as cheaply as the Portuguese do in his childhood neighborhood. His days would be filled with roaming the streets of Porto and teaching tourists about the architecture and culture. Which, of course, is something that he not only is passionate about, but has the requisite tools to teach.

Geoarbitrage is the process of making money in a high cost of living area and then moving to a low cost of living area.

Boom! Andy just started another climb. The possibilities are endless.

SUBSTITUTE WHEN ALL ELSE FAILS

Even if the above tools are not part of your toolbelt, this does not condemn you to an unhappy life. While I do believe that we have to eventually engage in the joy of addition to bring purpose and climbs into our lives, there is still benefit in becoming a master in subtraction—or at least substitution.

What do I mean by "substitution"?

If you are in a job that you hate but desperately need the money from, how can you change things up to improve your situation? There are several possibilities. You can see if you can switch teams or positions in your current job. Maybe what you truly loathe is your boss—can you substitute in a new one by working under someone else at the same firm? Possibly your boss is fine but the division is not suited to you, while another is. Are there options to move? Maybe the problem is your employer. Could you improve life by doing the same job for a new one?

I'm sure there is no lack of variables in your current job that I don't understand. The question becomes how you can manipulate those variables to make your life better. While substitution is less powerful than addition and subtraction, an avalanche of change starts with the simplest things. Creating margin in your life in even the smallest way can eventually lead to massive change for the better.

Can you substitute location? As we mentioned before, geoarbitrage can be an incredibly powerful tool. By changing neighborhoods, cities, or even countries, you might find that your money goes further. The less things cost, the less you have to make in a job that may not suit you.

Can you change how you spend? Substitute eating at home instead of eating out. Substitute homemade coffee instead of going to Starbucks. Substitute a discount grocery store instead of the high-priced one. Can you cancel subscriptions and find your news online? The key is not to get rid of things you truly enjoy but to manage wastefulness in order to create more margin. More space to breathe.

THE BEST THINGS IN LIFE ARE FREE

A dear friend of mine named Stephen has always dreamed of becoming a professional race car driver. He often laments that he would have been a serious contender except that he never had the funds to go to driving school. While that season of his life passed and he still does not have the funds, nothing precludes him from building a climb around it.

Climbs are malleable. There is more than one way to create a life brimming with them. There is nothing stopping Stephen from starting a racing blog or podcast. He could volunteer at the local speedway or try to get a job working for one of the major teams. He could create a local chapter or organization for race fans. There are ways to enjoy a passion without spending tons of money. The internet has created a marketplace for ideas and passions, as well as things that are mostly free or low cost.

It bears repeating: the best thing about a climb isn't the peak or destination; it is the enjoyment of the process. That enjoyment should be tightly tied to the people your climb introduces you to, and the community you build around it. Stephen will never receive the fame and accolades of winning the Indy 500, but he can get the same benefits by living a life he loves and connecting with people who have similar passions. These will be his people, and they will nurture him through good times and bad.

The same goes for being involved with activities that require gear. How many times have you seen people go out and buy expensive running shoes and high-tech heartrate monitors to psych themselves up to become a runner? Yet months later, all those material things are sitting in the closet unused. The way you become a runner is by running. It has nothing to do with the expensive stuff. If gear is absolutely necessary, there are so many used and secondhand marketplaces. Stop worrying about the gear and get involved in the activity!

TIME WON'T GIVE ME TIME

As much as we embrace a scarcity mindset with money, we are no better with time. Time scarcity is another common reason people believe there is no possibility of embracing a new climb. This complaint is especially echoed by those who feel they are at the fringes of making a living. They are too busy with their minimum wage jobs, working nights and weekends, and picking up extra shifts.

I admit that I have never walked in those shoes. I have never lived paycheck to paycheck and couldn't possibly know what that feels like. There is, however, scientific research that throws interesting light on the question. The data shows that the wealthy tend to work longer hours and have less free time. As Derek Thompson wrote in the *Atlantic*, there is a free-time paradox in America.[42] The rich were meant to have the most leisure time. The working poor were meant to have the least. But the opposite is happening.

While Thompson posits a number of reasons for this, the truth is that leisure time is more abundant than ever. According to analysis from the American Time Use Survey, Americans on average have more than five hours of free time a day.[43] The numbers are even higher for those with a low income or lower levels of education.

A lack of free time is not stopping people from pursuing their climbs.

WHY THE EXCUSES?

While money and time are not the only reasons people feel unable to pursue purpose in a meaningful way, they certainly magnify the contrast between those who are more and less privileged. Why should this be so? While I don't have scientific data to back this up, I do have a theory: it all comes back to happiness.

As we covered earlier in this book, happiness consists of both meaning and purpose. Meaning is how we interpret the past and hopefully start to feel like the hero of our own story. Purpose is about the present *and* the future.

If you are struggling to make ends meet, trapped in a job you don't love, it is hard to find meaning in past struggles. You end up having more of a victim mentality. Andy couldn't find a high-paying job because of the reckless banks whose greediness led to the great recession in 2008. The economy was in a shambles when he left college. Stephen couldn't race cars because his parents never had enough money to support him. The narrative we end up telling ourselves becomes clouded with negativity and loss.

If this is how you feel about your past, how can you feel positive about your present and future? It is hard to have an abundance mindset when everything in your life feels scarce. Instead of a virtuous cycle, it becomes a vicious cycle.

I don't blame you if you are in this exact place and feel like someone dropped you in a hole and removed the ladder. How are you supposed to be able to climb? I humbly offer two opinions. First, try to embrace a single tiny climb, no matter how small. Use a few spare moments to do something that fills you up. Make it a small reminder that there is something in this world that you can control and that gives you pleasure. Religiously protect this thing. Nurture and grow it whenever you develop a little bit of margin.

Second, apply narrative therapy. Though you may not be able to afford a therapist yourself, how can you evaluate the major negative narratives that affect the way you think about yourself? How can you examine them in such a way that you separate your own inherent goodness from the negativity or trauma surrounding events? Can you rewrite this story in such a way that, instead of being a victim, you become the victor?

The benefit of becoming aware of your purpose and practicing these climbs is not only your own happiness, but also the happiness of those around you. We often talk about the legacy we might leave behind based on the things we create, the records we break, and the money we make. In reality, legacy is deeper and more profound. It is mostly due to the people we have touched and the communities we have formed. As we will talk about in Part 3, there is no better way to do this than with little P purpose.

This is how you will change the world. But you have to believe that you can. You have to let go of the excuses.

A PURPOSE PRESCRIPTION: PERFORMING A TIME AUDIT

- Clear your schedule for an hour on two separate occasions in the next week. If you can, turn off all electronics or silence your phone. Find a quiet place where you will not be disturbed.

- We are going to create a time diary. There are several phone apps that you can download for free. Otherwise, you can use the old paper and pencil method. To make this audit less onerous, I suggest doing this on two separate days. I would also limit your tracking to the hour as opposed to the minute.

- On the days that you track, try to be honest about doing the activities that you normally do. This is not the time to draw any conclusions. You just want to create an accurate record.

- I suggest you wait at least seven days after your last tracking day before analyzing the data.

- Before getting deep into the data, give yourself a moment of grace. There is no reason every hour should be filled with productive activities. That would be exhausting.

- Now for the difficult part. For any given day, separate your productive hours from your nonproductive hours. Are you surprised by how much or how little you are accomplishing?

- How much free or leisure time do you have? Remember that the average American has five hours a day. How do you compare? What do you usually do during these leisure hours?

- Does your leisure time feel like time well spent? Are the activities you are involved in at the time regenerative, restful, or pleasurable? Would you classify any of this time as wasted?

- How much television do you watch? How much time is spent on social media? Do these minutes or hours add to your life or subtract from it?

- When was the last time you decided not to do something that you were interested in because you thought you didn't have enough time? Looking at your current time audit, was this in fact true?

- At the end of this exercise, how do you feel? Are you surprised by what you found? Are you upset? Does this new knowledge make you want to change any of your habits or activities?

- Again, there are no right or wrong answers here. My hope is that this audit will make time feel more concrete. Do you feel that time is abundant or scarce? If time feels scarce, how can you change this perception?

PART 3: SMALL BUT MIGHTY— HOW LITTLE P PURPOSE CHANGES THE WORLD

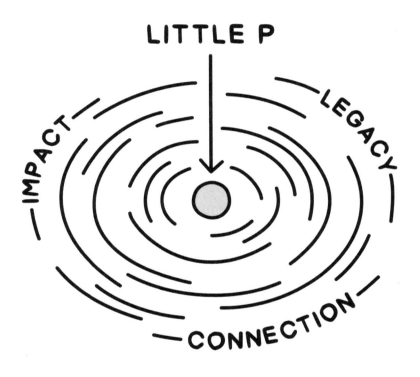

When we use the phrase "*little P*" to describe our sense of purpose, we are technically being a tad inaccurate. While the purpose may be small by our definition, the *potential* is anything but. It is, in fact, exponential. In Part 3 of this book, I will tell you why.

While big P purpose sounds outsized and audacious at first, in reality it fails to produce the kind of impact and legacy that we all hope for. This is counterintuitive. We have been told by our parents, social media, and society in general that we all need to be "killing it." Yet we so rarely clearly define what that means.

"Killing it" might mean making a lot of money, excelling at a job, or becoming famous. While these accomplishments feel grand when unexamined, taking a closer look will show that real and lasting impact comes from being our best selves and making deeper connections with the people around us, not producing Instagram-worthy moments that make our friends and followers jealous.

When I say "*legacy*," I am talking about the things you do today which last long after you have died, living on in the people who knew and loved you. To have this kind of impact, many mistakenly believe that you have to create some sort of social good or a large-scale personal improvement. You have to either win the Nobel Prize or become a billionaire.

As we know, however, these types of large-scale goals are usually unachievable. Though many will try, only as few as the top 1% will succeed. Does that mean that the bottom 99% leave this world as failures, having no impact or measurable legacy? We know that this is not how the world works. It just doesn't feel right! But if you place all your eggs in the basket of big P purpose, you are likely to fall into this trap. No wonder so many people are anxious.

Even those who do succeed in that way can see their work undone over time. Inventors create goods or products that are eventually supplanted by better ideas. The heirs of billionaires often lose all the family money within three generations—from shirtsleeves to shirtsleeves in just a few decades. This leaves us in a quandary.

How do we create legacy in a way that doesn't make us anxious, but also stands the test of time? How do we transmit the best of ourselves to the people that come after us?

The answer comes from an unexpected place. To better understand how we positively impact those that follow in our footsteps, we can glean quite a bit by studying how we *negatively* impact them. Theories of generational and genetic trauma have been well hashed out in various places.[44] While it is clear that the trauma we experience is often passed down many generations into the future, we rarely discuss how generational growth is *also* passed on. Legacy need not be damning.

Finally, we will return to the deathbed regrets. We will discuss how often these regrets center on our inability to accomplish the things that were really important to us. Yet if we dive deeper, we find that our biggest fear is that the lack of those accomplishments means we will not live on in the minds of those we love. We fear that we didn't impact them. We fear that the best parts of ourselves will disappear once our hearts stop pumping and our cells stop dividing.

What a relief it would be to know that we can live on. That hundreds of years from now, the successes of our descendants may be directly related to the legacy we leave today.

Does this sound too good to be true? Would you believe me if I told you that we all have the tools necessary to do just this? Legacy building, you'll find, is a lot less complicated and difficult than you expect.

Let's start Part 3 and I'll show you how.

CHAPTER 8:
HOW THE LITTLE P(URPOSE) SUPPORTS THE BIG P(EOPLE)

We have spent much of our time discussing big concepts like meaning, purpose, and happiness. Now I have to drop a bomb: I have misled you. I'm not kidding. I have spent the first two parts of this book convincing you to dissect these three concepts to build a better and happier life. The deception comes in the form of the true goal. Meaning and purpose are not the goal. Happiness is not the goal. What I really want for you is connections and communities. They are what winning truly looks like.

Why have I waited so long to say this? Simple. While connections, community, and legacy are arguably most impactful when it comes to fulfillment, they require the least work. The payoff in the end costs almost nothing! It is simply the natural product of building a life of little P purpose. As I said before, if you build it, they will come. The "*they*" that I am referring to are your connections, your community—your people.

This chapter starts out with an explanation of why people themselves cannot be purpose. Although at times we will feel we are living for our parents, spouse, or children, becoming our best self means developing a sense of purpose outside of them.

While people themselves can never be purpose, purpose does create strong bonds with those around us. When we intentionally engage in deeply meaningful activities, we find people with the same calling. We bond to these people through shared goals and interests. These people become our community.

It is in the building of community that we use purpose to establish legacy. We touch those around us and change them. And that change becomes like a pebble dropped into the ocean.

The effects of the water displaced can be felt for miles and miles.

PEOPLE ARE NOT YOUR PURPOSE

Juan was a family man. He immigrated to the United States to create more abundance for his wife and two small children. His goals were simple: build a business and move into a nice neighborhood. While these felt like audacious goals in the beginning, Juan had one big advantage. He was an amazing cook. His used this advantage to secure a job at a posh restaurant and then opened his own restaurant, which eventually became a chain.

Juan would freely admit that he didn't love cooking. He also had little interest in being an entrepreneur. He dreamed of being an artist or a dancer, but those things didn't pay the bills. A deeply ingrained drive to provide for his beloved family, however, motivated him to do things that he would normally avoid. He had not only made peace with his decisions, but truly enjoyed them.

Juan's restaurant chain became so successful that he was able to move his family into one of the best school districts in the city. His children never knew the deep and profound hunger that Juan had grown up with. Instead of playing in the local junkyard, as he had done, they had access to the best libraries, the most expensive exercise facilities, and the newest high-tech gadgets. Juan and his family were rich.

His wife didn't even have to work (though she spent as much time in the restaurants as he did). Instead, she volunteered for organizations and served on the kids' school board. She even used some of their profits to open up a homeless shelter and soup kitchen. There was so much work to be done. Juan sat at the head of a busy family, full of all the hustle and bustle of modern American life. He and his wife spent almost all their free time shuttling the kids to practice or afterschool tuition.

If you asked Juan at that time what his purpose was in life, his answer would be quick: "*Mi familia.*" His family. They were the reason he woke up in the morning and the reason he spent so many exhausting days at work. There could be no better reason to labor from sunrise to sunset. That is what good parents do.

Although the days were long, the years were short. First Juan's son and then his daughter went to college. Then he hired a new manager who was worth her weight in gold. She took all the time-consuming and bothersome activities off his hands. He could come in late and leave early. He didn't even have to show up on weekends.

This was the boon that Juan had been working for: enough money to support a fulfilling retirement, successful kids who were attending top universities, and a wife who was using every last moment to improve the world and give back to those in need. So why was he so unhappy? These should be his golden years.

Juan's problem is so common that we often don't recognize it as a problem. We have over-idealized the role of parents as grand sacrificers. And the reason we do this is called the **myth of joyful parenthood**.[45] This term arose from a study in 2011 conducted by two psychological scientists at the University of Waterloo. The study revealed an interesting contradiction: parents justified the significant emotional and financial investment in raising children by convincing themselves that the emotional rewards must be worth more than the numerous sacrifices, even if they didn't always feel those rewards directly.

Juan convinced himself that his children were purpose enough. As the years passed, however, the kids no longer needed him. They built lives of their own in which they no longer sought his physical help or even emotional support. They married and forged careers of their own—which left Juan out in the cold.

Even Juan's wife was so engaged in her own sense of purpose that she had little time for him. She was always running off to another gala or school board meeting, or raising funds for the shelter. His kids were always working or (eventually) taking care of their own children. Bored and unable to figure how to use all his newfound time, Juan returned to his business to find that it was running smoothly under the care of his skilled employees. He began to wonder why he had never pursued his childhood dreams of becoming a dancer. He regretted that it was too late for such things.

The problem with the Juans of the world is that they invest so much in future generations that they forget to invest in themselves. By doing this, they often create healthy, well-adjusted children who have the opportunity to build a sense of purpose of their own. But in the process, they rarely do the hard work of discovering their own individual sense of purpose and building a series of climbs around it.

People themselves cannot be your purpose. While I have focused on the parent-child example, this holds true for all sorts of other relationships. For similar reasons, our spouses, or grandchildren, or whoever else, should not be our purpose in life.

THE ULTIMATE ACT OF LOVE

Investing in ourselves is its own act of love for those important people in our lives. This wasn't lost on Juan's eldest son, Robert. Growing up tagging along with his father at work, Robert was exposed to many of the nurturing and selfless acts that Juan performed for him. He understood what it meant to be loved unconditionally and to be supported by his family. On the other hand, as far as his father was concerned, he lacked a role model for what being personally fulfilled looked like. Juan had no great love for his restaurants, and Robert recognized this quickly.

His father also had no interests, no hobbies, and no passions beyond caring for his family. This left Robert feeling a little disconnected. He understood the idea of making money and supporting those around him, but what did that mean to a college-educated young man with no wife or family? He found himself rudderless. Robert had no idea how to truly connect with the people around him or how to start creating the types of fulfilling climbs that would engage him for the rest of his adult life. His father hadn't modeled that.

The only thing he had an inkling to do was to get married and have children. But to whom?

Compare this to Juan's daughter, Cee Cee, who spent much more time with her mother growing up. She often accompanied her mom to volunteer at various organizations; and as a high schooler, she became her mom's campaign manager when she ran for the school board. Cee Cee witnessed firsthand how her mother filled her time with purposeful activities. These activities not only provided an opportunity to bond with her daughter, but also connected her to other people and her community.

Cee Cee's outlook as she went to university was very different from her brother's. Modeling after her mother, she joined a sorority, and within a few years became student president of the local chapter. She used this position to organize food drives and launch a campaign to clean up the campus. These activities were highly meaningful to her and connected her to a community of organizers, philanthropists, and mission-oriented individuals.

While Robert struggled to define what he wanted to do for a living, Cee Cee exited college with several job offers. Her sorority chapter head wanted her to work for the national organization. A number of charities that she worked with throughout her four-year tenure had seen her value and wanted to engage her as a fundraiser or administrator. And the master's degree she was considering came with a big fat scholarship.

The point of contrasting Robert and Cee Cee is not to suggest that sacrifice for one's family is a bad thing. But it is a poor model for developing a sense of purpose and meaningfulness in your child's life. Part of providing for them as children is not only economic but also spiritual and emotional.

We have mistaken love, in the form of material support, as a substitute for happiness. Cee Cee is more likely to find another human being to deeply connect with as an engaged young person with passions, ideas, and excitement. She is more likely to build a life with that person and have children. Those children are then more likely to learn from her modeling and build engaging lives themselves.

While Juan has brought Robert up to do whatever it takes to nurture his family, his wife has had a much more profound effect on Cee Cee. Her activities and passions not only nurture her daughter and her future grandchildren; they also affect the world around her. During Cee Cee's time as student president in her sorority, she helped to feed countless homeless people. She worked with other sororities and fraternities to beautify the campus, creating a more enjoyable environment for all the other students.

When we engage in purpose, we change not only ourselves but the people around us.

A HAPPY SIDE EFFECT

This is not to say that I believe changing the people around us should be a person's sole purpose. Much like Juan's fixation on family, focusing our sense of purpose outward instead of inward can have disastrous effects. While Cee Cee did much good in the world with her passion projects, it is important that those passions generally fit—at least roughly—into the climb framework.

This can be a tricky balance to strike. Cee Cee, growing up her mother's daughter, felt true joy in community organizing. She loved her memories of her parents' soup kitchen and of the fun she had creating campaign posters for her mother's school board runs. The joys were tied to a deep interest in the work she was doing—work that she shared with her mom. It was no wonder that, after graduating college, instead of taking a job with someone else, Cee Cee signed on with the soup kitchen and shelter her mom had invested so much time and love in.

Yet as she grew in the organization, Cee Cee left behind all the nurturing aspects she loved so much about helping other people, and instead became involved with administration and fundraising. As time passed, she found herself enjoying day-to-day activities less and becoming overly concerned about their potential impact. If they could only raise more money, they could feed more mouths and open more shelters.

Maybe they could solve the homeless crisis in the whole city!

These big audacious goals, while sounding fantastic when said out loud, created a template for failure. That template led to a series of daily activities which Cee Cee no longer felt connected to and a goal that was all but unreachable.

Cee Cee had turned her joyous climb into a big audacious anxiety-ridden goal. This was not at all what her mother had imagined lying on her deathbed when she directed the head of the charity's board to give Cee Cee the responsibility for running the shelter and food kitchen.

Does this sound familiar? "Cee Cee" is short for "Cilia," our sufferer of purpose anxiety from Chapter 1. By anchoring her climb in helping other people, instead of the joy of her moment-to-moment activities in the soup kitchen, she turned her little P purpose into a big audacious example of big P Purpose.

All of a sudden, instead of feeling nurtured, she was suffering from anxiety.

The better goal is if helping people is a happy side effect. Roman, the baseball card baron, never set out to change the lives of the nerdy teenagers who wandered into his store. His main climb was based on his love of baseball and his joy of buying and selling things. Yet the happy side effect was that he created a community and became a mentor. He formed a bulwark of safety and camaraderie that nurtured other people.

This is what happens when we authentically pursue purpose in a self-serving way. We inalterably touch the people around us.

Are you building communities?

COMMUNITIES OF INTERNAL PURPOSE

Understanding and pursuing our purpose will automatically lead to the formation of community. At its most basic, a community is a group of people who share a common characteristic or interest within society. We often become a part of communities without even thinking about it. They may, in part, be formed by our neighborhood, our socio-economic class, or the church we attend on Sunday.

The intensity of our bond to these communities depends on how significant a choice it was to become part of them, and how much time and emotion we invest in them on a regular basis. Definitional communities—those formed by an innate characteristic—are typically less tied to our passions. I may be part of the District 65 school system because my child goes to middle school down the street, but my participation is rather involuntary and being part of that particular district generally doesn't define me.

There are, however, other types of communities that play a more important role in our lives. These have been referred to as **communities of internal purpose**.[46] Unlike more external entities, these communities exist to take care of themselves and are made up of individuals who come together to support each other, learn, and grow. The idea is to foster a sense of fellowship and build deeper, more supportive relationships.

While being part of these internal communities sounds wonderful, are there any known benefits to this? The research is ongoing, but there have been some positive studies. A paper published in 2020 in *SSM - Population Health* found a relationship between a sense of community belonging and self-reported health at various life stages.[47] Furthermore, greater community engagement and social participation are associated with better health in old age and a significantly reduced risk of mortality.[48] Unbelievably, this may have as pronounced an effect as not smoking, drinking in moderation, exercising regularly, and maintaining a healthy diet. And finally, a study published in *Psychology* in 2022 showed that participation in various social organizations and communities increased retirees' subjective sense of wellbeing or happiness.

Taken together, the results of these studies should sound familiar. People involved in communities live longer, are healthier, and report a greater sense of happiness and wellbeing. The effects are exactly the same as those found for pursuing purpose in general.

Does that surprise you?

COMMUNITIES ARE EVERYTHING

Communities have come to mean everything to me. I only had this realization when I found the right ones—communities imbued with passion and purpose. The medical community did not fulfill this role for me. I felt disconnected and out of touch with other physicians because my identity was no longer being served by that sense of purpose. In many ways, I had outgrown it. I didn't make many physician friends or enjoy hanging out in places where you would find other doctors.

As I transitioned away from medicine, I found another community to be much more fulfilling. My interest in personal finance led me to the financial independence movement. This is a community that believes smart money and lifestyle management can lead to financial freedom: having enough money to do the things we really want to do without worrying about the price tag.

I immersed myself in this community by blogging and podcasting, joining online groups, and eventually meeting members in real life at conferences. Unlike with my doctor "friends," I felt a deep connection to this group of people. I found that we shared the same values and often had similar hopes and aspirations. I met people farther up on some of the climbs I was deeply interested in. They lent a hand or tossed down a lifeline to help me keep moving forward. I also interacted with those who were a few steps behind. They were struggling with terrain that I had just passed through. I had plenty of helpful tips and tricks to help them along the way.

I began to grow in ways that I never expected. My lifelong wish to become an author and publish a book went from an out-of-reach dream to concrete reality. My community connected me to people who had already succeeded at such things. They were not only experienced in treading the paths that I was beginning to explore, but happy to offer advice and connect me to other helpful people.

Thousands of small life changes have also come from being part of a community. I now have friends and connections in many major cities around the world. I have people who I can call on to meet in a foreign land and bring a sense of comfort to an adventure. I have people!

As a brief example, just the other day I was driving from Chicago to one of my favorite community events in Minnesota: Camp Financial Independence. This is a weekend-long meeting where likeminded individuals discuss their finances, life goals, and tips and tricks to being more intentional with money. Driving down Highway 94, I realized that one of my acquaintances—who I had met at the same conference four years earlier—happened to live in a town a few hours away on my intended route. Julie and I had spent maybe a couple of hours together in person in total and exchanged fewer than a half-dozen text messages over the last year. This didn't stop me from Facebook-messaging her in the middle of the trip to see if she was available to share a meal. Her answer was spontaneous and before I knew it, I had plans to stop at her house, meet her boyfriend, and eat a delicious and healthy homemade meal. We shared not only a great conversation, but the joy of being in the presence of other people who share our values and goals.

How lucky am I? How lucky could you be? These momentary chances to connect have helped me create a life that I feel deeply engaged in—a life full of exciting events and chance occurrences which fill my time with joyful activities. Being part of a community is the ultimate abundance. We have countless ways to learn, grow, and have fun—together.

HOW TO BECOME A COMMUNITY MEMBER

We should not be daunted by the goal of community formation and participation. Most of the time, the biggest driver of being a successful member comes from our inner interest in the community itself, its members, and the purpose that causes the group to be formed in the first place. I liked the ideas behind the financial independence community and was enamored with the personal qualities of the people who introduced me to it. If we are intentional concerning our attempts, becoming part of various communities should be a walk in the park. Here are some suggestions about how you might go about doing that:

- **Become your best you:** I will not belabor the point because we have discussed and will continue to discuss the idea that pursuing a life of little P purpose will automatically connect you to many different communities. The more entrenched you are in joyful activities in which you enjoy the process of doing, the more people you will attract around you. This becomes a *de facto* community.
- **Build what you want to see in the world:** One presenter at this year's Camp Financial Independence discussed how his room-mate would go to the gym every morning at 5:30 am and talk to every person who was there working out at such an early hour. He decided that anyone mad enough to be there so early must be his type of person. He invited every single one of them to his apartment for lunch that day. Some came and some didn't. He repeated this several days a week for the next month. Before he knew it, he had a regular group of lunch buddies who could talk endlessly about working out, time optimization, and the joy of waking up early.

- **Sign up for a class:** Do you like landscape painting? How about baking delicious pastries? Could you afford to take a class to learn more? Enrolling in activities that are joyful for you will bring you that much closer to being part of a community. You will be bonded not only by common interests, but also by being in a similar place on the climb. As you grow and change together, you will find the people as pleasing as the activity.
- **Volunteer:** Opportunities to volunteer at hospitals, soup kitchens, Meals on Wheels, or other organizations are myriad. Organizations are often looking for an extra set of hands to pitch in and make a difference. This is a great way to pay tribute to a difficult time in your own past or support a cause that is important to a family member. You will not only derive benefit from helping other people but also be in the same place at the same time with those who share some of your values.
- **Become a fan:** Do you love Taylor Swift? The Chicago Bears? Do you feel passionate about the session ale produced in the taproom at your favorite brewery? Why not become a fan? Online forums, organized events, and clubs are all formed to attract people who have the same interest as you. Even if you are totally introverted, there are ways to interact online and only when you feel up for it.

I could go on. There are countless ways to find communities to become a part of. All the search requires is one thing: you have to take action. A community is not going to just find you. You have to create one or get off your duff and find one. The best things in life may not cost money, but you will have to expend some energy.

WE CHANGE THE WORLD
THROUGH OTHER PEOPLE

We began this chapter by making the argument that other people cannot be our purpose. True growth requires that we develop a sense of self outside of those we love and then pursue those activities that we find innately joyful. This is little P purpose. This does not mean, however, that other people are not a big part of the equation.

Other people, in fact, are everything. We create purpose in our lives to connect to people in the form of communities. Communities nurture us and help us grow. They help us translate past meaning into present and future actions that engage us in our everyday life regardless of the goals and consequences.

The benefits run even deeper than just our own inner happiness or sense of wellbeing. As we will see in the next chapter, the pursuit of purpose and the creation of communities profoundly affect not only the people around us, but also their friends, acquaintances, and even kids.

These effects can last for years, decades—even generations.

I'm talking legacy here. Let's move on to Chapter 9 and I'll show you how we can build a lasting legacy that will long outlive us. After, of course, a quick exercise to make the most of what you learned in this chapter …

A PURPOSE PRESCRIPTION:
PERFORMING A COMMUNITY AUDIT

- Clear your schedule for an hour on two separate occasions in the next week. If you can, turn off all electronics or silence your phone. Find a quiet place where you will not be disturbed.

- Take a blank sheet of paper and draw a straight line, separating it into two halves. It does not matter if the lines are horizontal or vertical.

- On one side, write down all the communities you are part of that you did not choose. These might be based on where you live, the religion you were born into, your country of origin, or the language you speak at home.

- On the other side, list all the communities you choose to be a part of. Examples may be the university you attended, the sports team or athletic club you belong to, or other communities based on hobbies, interests, or joys.

- Circle any you consider to be communities of internal purpose—ones that exist to take care of themselves and that are made up of individuals who come together to support each other, learn, and grow.

- Do you feel more or less connected to the communities you chose versus the ones you didn't? Are the communities of internal purpose fundamentally different than the others? How?

- How has being part of these communities changed your life? Have they connected you to new friends or introduced mentors whose advice has been particularly impactful?

- Now think about some of your current anchors of little P purpose that you have been considering since you started reading this book. Are there groups, meetings, or fan clubs related to people who share the same interest as you? If so, how would you go about finding them? What is holding you back?

- Finally, turn over the piece of paper and write down a list of five or ten communities you might be interested in becoming a part of. Would joining these communities be a good use of your time? Would you be your most authentic self around these types of people?

Connecting with others and being a good community member is like anything else: a muscle that grows when used and atrophies when ignored. Although meeting a bunch of strangers may sound anxiety-provoking, the long-term benefits far outweigh the risks. When we connect with other people around our sense of purpose, we are much more likely to affect them in profound ways that create a long-lasting legacy. Let's move on to the next chapter to explore this concept further.

CHAPTER 9:
A PEBBLE IN THE VAST OCEAN

A few years ago, I had the pleasure of hosting renowned financial therapists (and father and son) Brad and Ted Klontz as guests on my *Earn & Invest* podcast. During the conversation, Ted told a story of generational trauma that had permeated his family's life. He recalled struggling to make money in his earlier years, often working several jobs at a time. He remembered being on the cusp of falling asleep one evening and feeling frustrated at his lack of progress, but then the most interesting thought popped in his mind: "At least they can never call me lazy!"

As Ted explored what had prompted this thought, he learned more about his family history. His great-grandfather had come to America from Ireland with his two sisters and had never succeeded financially. In fact, his great-grandfather died in a poorhouse. Other family members attributed his lack of success to laziness. Fast forward to his maternal grandfather: facing down the Great Depression, he worked in a legendary fashion from dawn to dusk, holding multiple jobs at the same time, to save the family farm.

Ted was flabbergasted. He was suffering through the mishaps of his ancestors, and those mishaps were having a profound effect on his sense of success, wellbeing, and happiness. When it comes to wealth accumulation, Ted and Brad created a framework to understand this generational trauma, coining the term "**money scripts**" to describe core beliefs about money that drive financial behavior.

There are four types of money scripts:

- money avoidance;
- money worship;
- money status; and
- money vigilance.

What does this have to do with purpose and legacy building? In this chapter, we will flip the script and discuss not only how poor coping behaviors come from past trauma, but also how we can inherit growth and abundance-oriented scripts that help us become better, happier, and more adapted. Now, don't worry. As we have previously discussed, using tools like narrative therapy can help overcome poor coping skills if you have them. And just because you haven't inherited any of these generational growth scripts, doesn't mean you can't write them anew (with little P purpose)—and pass them down.

Money scripts are your unconscious beliefs about money, often rooted in childhood, that affect your adult behaviors and perspectives.

What if the model you provide for friends and family is one not of fear (like Ted's money script), but of intentional living, filled with purpose and joy? Could this same script be gifted forward from generation to generation so that, decades or centuries later, the positive actions of your descendants are the results of your actions today?

Like a ripple created by a pebble dropped in the ocean, could the water displaced ebb and flow for many years and miles? Could it build at points and recede at others, but never quite disappear altogether? This is the legacy you create by pursuing purpose. You are standing on the edge of the sandy beach with the pebble in the palm of your hand.

Are you ready to cast the pebble?

GENERATIONAL TRAUMA

Generational trauma is when trauma extends from one generation to the next for a person or group of people who undergo economic, cultural, or familial distress. Although the trauma is suffered by groups of people in one time or place—think the Holocaust, the Great Depression, or the flu pandemic of the early 20th century—the anxiety, fear, and depression are passed down to their descendants. Many believe that trauma traverses generations through actual genetic changes. They call this **epigenetics**.

The idea is that trauma changes how your genes work. Those genetic alterations are then inherited by your children.[49]

These changes manifest themselves in young people in the form of anxiety, depression, and even post-traumatic stress syndrome.[50] And most importantly, as with Ted and Brad Klontz's money scripts, they result in poor coping behaviors that lead to the exact opposite of what people want for themselves. Ted was not being served by his anxiety and workaholism. The survival of his family was not dependent on him being engaged in productive activities every single minute of the day.

These arguments about generational trauma are anything but theoretical. I can trace several through my own family lines. I am descended from a grandmother who emigrated to the United States from Syria in the early 1900s. Her mother was a victim of the flu pandemic in 1918 and her father was unable to take care of all his children alone. My grandmother, Sophie, was shipped off to an orphanage and spent most of her childhood and adolescence in a group home, which took care of her despite the Great Depression and the Wall Street crash.

Is it any wonder that Sophie turned into an adult with a scarcity mindset? Would you blame her for always having extra portions at the dinner table even though she wasn't particularly hungry? Imagine how she must have felt about money or about working. Sophie prided herself on saving and rarely spent on herself. What if it all disappeared and the bad times returned?

My mother, growing up as Sophie's child, inherited similar tendencies, having seen them modeled by her beloved mother. When tragedy struck and my father died, leaving my mother with three kids and one income, her scarcity tendencies were exacerbated. She even told us as children of her plan to sell the family house so that she could pay for our college educations. She planned to move herself into a small apartment in an inexpensive area if need be.

Even in the face of abundance, the scarcity script remained. After my mother had remarried and built up a very successful accounting practice, her fears about running out of money lingered even as her bank account grew. I remember one of our biggest arguments in childhood was over whether to go to an expensive restaurant to celebrate a sibling's high-school graduation. Although the cost would have absolutely no effect on the family finances, it became an emotional and traumatic decision for my mother. She was replaying generational trauma which had begun several decades before she was born.

Understanding this context helps me view my own money issues through a different lens. No wonder the idea of not having a regular paycheck is so stressful. No matter how many times I calculate the numbers and realize that I have enough money to continue living my current life, doubts arise. I am genetically, or at least generationally, prone to feeling the effects of scarcity even when they are not there.

This is a hurdle that I have to overcome. Many of us have similar hurdles, depending on the traumas suffered by our ancestors. None of us escape unscathed. Although not the subject of this book, healing generational trauma is possible through recognition, self-care, and therapy (narrative and otherwise). All is not lost. And what if, instead of passing on only the traumas we endure, we could also pass on all our triumphs? What if we could pass on all the good things too?

Well, I believe we can.

GENERATIONAL GROWTH

If you Google the term "generational growth," you'll find a number of websites that deal with investing capital and passing on money to your children and grandchildren. But this can be done with more than money. Future generations can benefit from our positive experiences.

I have already documented a few of these examples of generational growth from my childhood. But there were countless others. In fact, some were even apparent in the baseball cards that Roman and I bonded over when I was a little kid. There was Cal Ripken Sr. and Cal Ripken Jr.; Bobby Bonds and Barry Bonds; Ken Griffey Sr. and Ken Griffey Jr. Each of these father-and-son pairs of highly successful professional baseball players demonstrates how not only physical talent but also a sense of community and connections can be passed on.

I imagine the same is true of you. Have you ever recognized a positive trait or interest of your own and tried to trace it back to one of your parents or grandparents? Have you ever been told that you inherited a skill, attitude, or even intelligence from someone that came before you?

I certainly have. I love math. I always have. I had a learning disability that affected almost every aspect of childhood learning, but my mathematical abilities were spared. Somewhere deep down inside, I knew that my issues with reading couldn't be from stupidity because then I would be bad at math also. This belief was my saving grace. All those years I was behind my classmates in almost every subject; but I was faster and better at addition and multiplication. That was enough.

My love affair with math should be of little surprise. My mom loves math too. She started her career as a chemist, but ultimately went back to school to become a certified public accountant. She is a master of all things QuickBooks and Microsoft Excel; a whiz at tax returns. Not only is she really good at numbers, but they form the core of some of her most joyful activities. My mom retired a number of years ago and still attends regular continuing education classes to keep on top of the field.

She may not need to use math in her professional life anymore, but she finds these types of pursuits a good way to fill up her time—kind of sounds like a climb, doesn't it?

The story doesn't end there. You know who also was an accountant? My maternal grandfather. My mother remembers sitting on his lap as a kid as he pored through the financial reports and tax returns of his clients. He would point out each column and explain to her what the numbers meant and how they interacted with each other to give him the information he needed.

This is generational growth. Just as trauma can be passed down to those who come after us, so too can joyful and engaging beliefs, loves, and skills. I never met my maternal grandfather; he died of lung cancer before I was born. Yet I am fairly certain that his love of math has intimately touched my life. Because of him, I had the confidence not only to survive my learning disability, but also to pursue a highly mathematical career. My interest and abilities in math helped me conquer the highly technical courses that were necessary to pursue a pre-med curriculum. As a hospice doctor, every day I have to convert one type of medication to another, which often requires me to do complex mathematical equations on the spot.

Furthermore, leaving medicine was predicated on my involvement in the financial independence movement. For instance, to understand how to calculate a 4% withdrawal rate, I had to feel fairly comfortable with complex math.

Can you see how this type of thinking becomes exponential? As a doctor, think about how many lives I have affected. I remember once noting a mathematical association between two lab results of one of my patients. That connection, missed by many others, was caught based on my love of all things mathematical and led to a rare diagnosis. We were able to treat the patient with a simple medication and saved him the pain of many hospitalizations—possibly even death.

How many people would have been bereft if that man hadn't been in their lives? It turned out that my patient was a pastor at a local church. He often donated as much as 30% of his excess cash to causes such as the Red Cross and local foodbanks. He also provided safety and comfort for parishioners in need. He still does today.

A direct line can be drawn between my grandfather's love of math and the wellbeing of a runaway child searching for shelter at a local church. These lines span almost a full century as well as thousands of miles of distance. How incredible is that? Can you imagine what my grandfather would think if he knew how broad and enduring his legacy would be?

One of the biggest arguments for big P Purpose is that, if achieved, those big audacious goals change the lives of more than just one person. Curing cancer or solving the climate crisis would help millions. Becoming a billionaire could provide wealth for our descendants for centuries to come. All of this is true, even though the odds of succeeding are small.

But my grandfather's simple love of mathematics shows that you don't need big audacious goals to have big audacious impact. My grandfather was no superhero. You will find him in none of the lists of the most influential Americans from the 20th century. The number of people who know his name is falling as the decades pass. Yet he still lives on.

You can live on too.

PURPOSE AND LEGACY

The best way to create a legacy, as in the examples above, is by investing more in purpose by creating your own climbs. As you will note, my grandfather wasn't enthralled by math because he was thinking about how his grandson would eventually become a doctor. He didn't have a grandson at the time. Instead, he did what he was passionate about.

Of all the ways my mother could and did emulate him, why was it math that stuck with her?

My grandfather was most alive and intentional when he was looking at spreadsheets and solving complex problems. He was most himself. As a child, my mother would have noted this both consciously and subconsciously. She would try on his identity to see if it fit her. Did she get as much joy from numbers as he did? This process of testing and probing is often the first step children take in the process of **individuation**—that is, building their unique identity. They are constantly assessing the behavior of their parents and trying to decide what connects with them.

I don't think this testing is limited to parents. As children, we constantly evaluate the behavior of adults and children around us. We find role models and mentors outside the household. That was my experience with Roman. Although he was not a parent, he was an adult that I trusted. In many ways, I wanted to be like him. So, I tried on his behaviors. Would it surprise you to know that one of my first money-making ventures as a kid was to buy and sell baseball cards? I modeled after my stepfather who owned a business buying and selling coins—and, of course, Roman.

Years later, I realized that the process of trying on that identity wasn't as enthralling as being a doctor. My baseball-card-selling days were short-lived. The tendency to buy and sell, however, has popped up at various times in my life. For a few years, I bought and sold artworks online. These were temporary climbs that were gratifying for short periods. Eventually, I outgrew them and focused my attention elsewhere.

I also patterned myself after fellow children. Remember that snarky teenager Ryan who worked for Roman? I wanted to be just like him. When Ryan went to college, I hoped to replace him in the antique store. It is only now, after many years, that I realize that Roman wisely picked another boy because he was having troubles at home.

The same can be said today. One of the reasons I finally became an author, after years of yearning, is that I built a community around myself which included several successful authors that I could emulate. Some of them even gave me advice.

Can we model behavior for our children and friends that *isn't* authentic—that is not imbued with little P purpose? While I believe that it is possible, I don't think it is as enduring. We can tell when a person is engaged in an activity that lights them up. We can sense the difference in their posture, their bearing, the air that surrounds them. It is hard to fake enthusiasm, and it is especially hard to fool kids.

Ask any highschooler about this. They will immediately be able to tell you which teachers are most enthusiastic about their subjects: they will generally be teaching the student's favorite classes. I was a science major who loved math, yet two of my favorite childhood classes were US history and Spanish. The reason had nothing to do with the subjects. It was the teachers. Mr. Rogan and Mr. McKinney engaged the kids in ways that others didn't. Their passion for their subjects and for teaching was unparalleled. Years later, I may not be a history buff or a fluent Spanish speaker, but I do consider myself a teacher.

One could counter that my own father's modeling contradicts this. I became a doctor to be just like my dad, but being a doctor did not serve me in the long term. Two thoughts come to mind here. One, my pursuit of medicine was just as much a product of the traumatic event of losing him as it was of watching him doing the job itself. Although my father loved practicing, I wasn't old enough to follow him around on the job. I wasn't modeling his behavior; I was trying to cope with his loss. I mistakenly thought that becoming a doctor would do that.

Two, I did often see my father engage in *other* purposeful activities. He was a master photographer, a lover of languages, and a tinkerer. He used to spend countless weekends in the basement surrounded by tools creating stuff. And it was this side of my father that really stuck with me. He was always engaged in some climb or another, and most used both his intellectual and creative skills together. If my dad were alive today, he would love podcasting. I might have to compete with him for an audience!

HOW TO BECOME PURPOSEFUL ABOUT LEGACY

To mangle a quote from the movie *Fight Club*: **the first rule of legacy building is—we don't talk about legacy**. Legacy is a byproduct of living a purposeful life and engaging authentically in these climbs. Similarly, when we talk about connections and community, our efforts should be based on building purpose and allowing the rest to flow naturally.

There are, however, some important considerations when it comes to having your purpose impact your family and others.

Live Out Loud

When it comes to bringing up children, many are great at involving their offspring in the nuts and bolts of daily life. We show them how we balance the checkbook and clean the garage, and we might even teach them about the stock market. We realize the benefits of modeling and are thoughtful about demonstrating important skills and activities. Yet when it comes to our sense of purpose and hobbies, we do it in the dark.

We manage these activities on our own time. We pursue them outside the home or wait until the kids have gone to sleep or are at school. If we want our children to have a healthy sense of purpose, we need to bring them along with us, as Marie did with Cilia in the soup kitchen. They need to see us intentionally engaged as our authentic selves, doing things that are important to us.

Create Communities

Our friends and family—and maybe even complete strangers—need to see us doing the things we are passionate about too. The way to do this is to build communities around yourself while doing these things. Love craft beer? Maybe you should start a social club for other craft beer drinkers that tours local breweries every month and samples their latest creations. Dreaming of running a marathon and feel like exercise is a major anchor for your sense of purpose? Try starting a blog or podcast to serve other people aspiring to accomplish the same dream as you.

How and where you start these communities is not important. Some may be virtual; others may be in person. The important thing is to bind yourself to other people who have similar interests to you. In doing so, you become a mentor to those less skilled than you and a student of those more skilled.

Volunteer

There is no better way to create a legacy than by volunteering at something you are passionate about. Remember Sarah from Chapter 3, who was trying to spend more time around the stables? One afternoon, she was able to volunteer with a group of Down's syndrome children who were brought by a local organization to the stables to learn how to ride. She had such a fun time that she sought out other ways to help this very special community.

She volunteered to help in countless other ways too, and even found herself babysitting for busy mothers and fathers who needed a break. Sarah's persistence, quick smile, and patience proved a godsend. Years later, she found herself receiving invitations to graduation parties and weddings. They remembered how helpful she was, long after her sense of little P purpose had moved her in a different direction.

Offer Services for Free

Andy, from Chapter 7, had a talent for fixing bikes. While he never made a go at fixing them as a business, he offered his services for free on race days. Not only did this give him a chance to watch a sport he loved, but he made a lot of friends along the way. Younger riders watched closely as he adjusted the gears and calibrated the tires. Several of them learned how to do most of the fixes themselves.

Andy never tried to hide his knowledge. The money a number of these kids saved with what they learned allowed them to maintain their bikes well past their expiration dates. One of those kids used this to convince his mother and father to allow him to keep racing even though they thought it too expensive. That kid is now the main designer for a well-known bike company and was once an alternate rider for the Tour de France. None of this would have happened if not for Andy.

Generational Growth and Generational Trauma Both Relate to Happiness

Aspiring to generational growth will not assure happiness. Yet it is one of the ways that we can positively act in the here and now. If you remember, we talked about happiness as the sum of meaning and purpose. Generational growth is very much about purpose. It relegates itself to both the here and now and the future. When we live out our purpose, it not only makes today better but also provides a chance to create a lasting legacy.

Generational trauma, however, is much more about meaning. It is about the past stories we tell ourselves about ourselves. It is about how we cognitively deal with the struggles of our past—not only our own struggles, but those of our ancestors. In order to overcome these struggles and find peace in the present, we must learn to reinterpret our past. This, again, is the domain of narrative therapy.

How do we rewrite the stories of the past and separate ourselves from harmful scripts given to us in childhood? How do we break the traumatic cycle?

While this book focuses more on purpose, the present, and the future, it is important to address the past. Overcoming generational trauma should be done with a skilled therapist trained in such activities. This is not a job for novices. Hiring a therapist is an investment in your future. Our ability to generate generational growth assumes that we can see our past as positive, and the result of our own heroic actions.

In the next chapter, we will discuss the issue of regret. Being present with people as they die has exposed me to much generational growth and trauma. The better we manage these, the less regret we will face as the end of life draws near. Although regret may follow us through our lives, it becomes most acute toward the end.

The best time to address regret is now, not sometime in the future.

Not when you are retired or have enough money. And certainly not on your deathbed. In Chapter 10, we will focus on the relationship between purpose and regret. As you can imagine, it all depends on which type of purpose you pursue.

A PURPOSE PRESCRIPTION:
PERFORMING A GENERATIONAL AUDIT

- Clear your schedule for an hour on two separate occasions in the next week. If you can, turn off all electronics or silence your phone. Find a quiet place where you will not be disturbed.

- For this exercise, all that is needed is a clear and open mind. You might, however, want to keep a notebook handy. Some of the issues that come up may be worth writing down for later.

- Close your eyes and think about the three things that you are most talented at or love the most. Your own skill is not as important as how much these activities or abilities mean to you. A large list may come to mind, but I want you to hone the list down to three concrete examples. What makes you feel most alive?

- For each talent, think back to your parents, grandparents, aunts, and uncles. Do any of them share the same skill? Remember the first time you became aware of this activity. Did you witness someone engaged in this climb before you? Did you inherit it? If so, did *they* inherit it from an even older ancestor? How far back can you trace this ability? Does it run in your family?

- Now, let's do the same thing, but concentrate on three limiting beliefs or negative self-perceptions. What are your most negative beliefs about yourself? What is the story you tell yourself about your own inability to live the way you want to live or accomplish the things you want to accomplish? Are you bad with money? Not motivated enough? Less athletic than everyone else?

- Before going any further, this is a good place to take some deep, cleansing breaths. Confronting your own negative self-talk can create anxiety and angst. As you concentrate on your breathing, let the bad feelings wash over you and fall to the wayside.

- Can you also trace these negative feelings to other people in your life? Do you remember your mother or father feeling the same way? Did their words or actions make you question your own safety or sense of worth?

- You have now done an inventory of three generational growth scripts and three generational trauma scripts. How do you feel? Do you find yourself feeling grateful or annoyed? Maybe a little of both?

Although we can't undo the generational effects of what our ancestors experienced, we can recognize how their struggles affect the way we operate years after they have passed. This recognition may help us break the trauma cycle.

We can also be thankful to our forebears for pursuing and embracing purpose in their lives. This purpose has created a positive legacy that has had a profound impact on who we are. Take a moment to think what you would like your legacy to be for future generations. Are you acting accordingly today by pursuing your purpose?

CHAPTER 10:
EMBRACE PURPOSE, ERASE REGRET

can tell you many heartbreaking stories of regret that I heard at the bedsides of my dying hospice patients: tales of loves lost, mistakes made, and opportunities abandoned. No matter the flavor, the taste is always bitter. No one wants to look back at their lives and wish they had behaved differently—acted with more courage and insight. Yet that is exactly what most of us do. Like purpose, regret is often a four-letter word.

For most of my hospice patients, it is unfortunately too late. Given their poor physical health and lack of time, it is unlikely we can help them overcome these regrets. Better instead to equip them to cope psychologically. If, by some lucky chance, resolution is possible, we celebrate the last-minute plot twist that saves the day. Unfortunately, *deus ex machinas* are few and far between. Many die grieving their inability to go back in time and make things right.

For those not on their deathbeds, however, regret can be not only bearable, but a great motivator to living a more fulfilled life.

Regret can be a gift.

To understand why, we need to delve into the relationship between regret, purpose, and happiness. Believe it or not, they are intimately connected. Few escape this life without dealing with regret. The key is not to avoid the discomfort, but rather to use it as a springboard to propel yourself to greater, happier heights.

How do we do this? How can regret add to our sense of wellbeing, instead of subtracting? To further elucidate this tricky relationship, I would like to introduce you to two women. Although they are separated by age, personality type, location, and stage of life, Beatriz and Christine share one essential characteristic: extreme regret was their first stop on the road to happiness.

And that road was paved with purpose.

BEATRIZ'S STORY

"I started making jewelry when I learned that I was dying."

At first, I thought I must have heard wrong. The beautiful brooch and necklace lying on Beatriz's nightgown were just two of many pieces displayed in her bedroom. It was my initial home visit and hospice evaluation, and I knew little about Beatriz's life. When I questioned her further, she chuckled at my confusion.

"I started making jewelry the *first* time I learned that I was dying."

Exactly 60 years ago to the month, Beatriz had gone to hospital with lower abdominal pain and a mass protruding from her belly. After a full week in hospital and countless tests, she was given the grim news. At just 30 years old, she appeared to have an extensive gynecological cancer that could be neither resected nor cured. She was sent home with well wishes and a return appointment in a few months, which no one expected she would be alive to attend.

Beatriz and her husband, shocked and saddened at the horrendous news, decided to make the best of the time that she still had left. They escaped to their summer cottage and dug in for whatever the future would bring. After just one short week, Beatriz became disenchanted. It was not like her to sit around and wait for death to come. Furthermore, she found herself considering that she was going to die with one really big regret.

She loved jewelry. Loved it so much that she always considered that one day she would become a designer herself. It was the dream that she clung to late at night. She could remember her own glamorous grandmother and playing dress-up in her room, borrowing her elaborate necklaces and bracelets. But this dream had never turned into reality.

Of course, Beatriz had planned to go to classes and learn, but she found her time fleeting at the beginning of her marriage. She had a house to maintain and a husband to take care of. There never seemed to be time or money. There was always another meal to prepare or social gathering to attend. Time passed and nothing changed.

Beatriz's death sentence, however, reignited the fire. *If not now, then when?* She was not going to waste what little time she had left. She hurried to the local arts and crafts store and picked up every imaginable bead, clasp, and chain she could get her hands on. She went to the library and checked out dozens of books. Given that she didn't know how much time she had left, Beatriz jumped down the rabbit hole of jewelry making with the abandon of someone who had few cares and nothing to lose. Because she truly *did* have nothing to lose.

Within a month, she had made her first few necklaces. Within three months, she had sold out everything in stock. Within a year, she had an exclusive deal with the local department store.

Meanwhile, something even more amazing happened: Beatriz didn't die. The diagnosis must have been wrong! She had been so busy that she hadn't bothered to go back to see her doctors. When she eventually did, they could find no evidence of any tumor.

With today's medical knowledge, it is clear that Beatriz was probably misdiagnosed. The quality and availability of scans at that time were poor to say the least. I am not suggesting that finding a sense of purpose caused a miracle—at least not a medical miracle.

Sixty years later, Beatriz had become one of the most sought-after jewelry makers in the world. And all thanks not only to a misdiagnosis, but something even more important: regret.

CHRISTINE'S STORY

It took a moment for me to process the melancholy words spoken by the well-attired young woman who was sitting on my examining table. Christine spoke evenly as she recounted the events that changed her life: the morning she, a careless 20-year-old, got into her car to drive to school and returned home a drastically different person.

Of course, she hadn't meant any harm. Christine would never hurt another human being—not on purpose. Although her parents had warned her about drinking and driving, no one had ever told her of the dangers of mobile phones. After all, she could text with her eyes closed—or so she thought.

She never forgot the feeling of the body as it bounced against her car. The blood that soaked her shoes as she jumped out to investigate. The look of the poor child's parents in court.

These are the things that stay with you.

I was gripped as she continued her story. I felt not only great sympathy but a strange sense of empathy (as a physician, I often felt responsible for my patients' deaths). After the accident, she had to come to terms with her immense sense of regret. She took stock of her life. She neither granted herself forgiveness nor wallowed in self-pity. But she did change just about everything. She developed a completely new sense of purpose.

A few years later, she had become a national spokesperson, lecturing around the country on the dangers of texting and driving. The loss of one life ignited the courage to save countless others.

Deep and profound regret had been joined by something that Christine wasn't sure that she deserved. But she would hold on to it no matter what happened in the future.

REGRET COMES IN TWO FLAVORS

Regret is a feeling of sadness or remorse over a past action, decision, or choice. While Beatriz and Christine's stories center on this, they are not identical. Their differences shed light on the main types of regret that people are likely to suffer from. It turns out that regret generally comes in two flavors. Neither tastes particularly good. Most of us will experience both.

The first kind is **inaction regret**. These are regrets of omission—the types of things that I talk about with my dying patients. They never had the energy, courage, or time to do things that were deeply important to them. Analysis paralysis often drives this, when we come up with every reason in the world not to do something that is important to us. This is very much what happened to Beatriz. It was only the (ultimately false) specter of her looming death that spurred her into action.

The second type of regret is **action regret**. This relates to actions that have disastrous consequences which cannot be undone. Those consequences are often unforeseen at the time of the action. Christine had no idea, when she got in her car that day, that the act of texting while driving would cost someone's life. After the fact, she would have done anything to go back in time and not have taken the action. But it was too late. The cascade of events had taken place and was now unalterable.

The relationship between inaction and action regret and purpose and happiness is slightly different in each case. Inaction regret is very present and future focused. Because of this, we do not necessarily have to look back at the past and assign a sense of meaning to these activities. Action regret, on the other hand, focuses not only on the present, but also the past. We have to come to terms with what came first in order to pursue a sense of purpose today.

INACTION REGRET

Inaction regret is the kind I most often encounter in the dying. The examples are too numerous to count. Whether it be the hobby unpursued, the book unwritten, or the relationship unrepaired, we are often saddened by those important things we somehow chose not to do. These regrets are universal. The excuses for not achieving what we wanted to achieve are myriad. I believe we are often disingenuous when we blame money and time. The real reasons often center on not only the fear of failure but also the emotional work needed for deeply important activities. We place endless obstacles in our way to avoid that hard work.

Beatriz is a perfect example. There was nothing truly stopping her from pursuing her dream of making jewelry before her diagnosis. Whether she would have admitted it to herself or not back then, she was forthright in her deathbed conversations 60 years later. "I was scared to death of failure!"

These fears give us an excuse to delay until a better time. We come up with all sorts of reasons for putting something off until tomorrow. Weeks become months and months become years. If we are unlucky, we find ourselves admitted to hospice without ever throwing our hat in the ring. We never even enter the arena.

While inaction poses serious regrets for the dying, it doesn't have to for the living. As Beatriz accidently discovered, assessing regrets can become a great template for building climbs. In fact, the only way to truly extinguish an inaction regret is to build a successful climb around it.

This simple step can be taken by anyone. The key is to recognize regrets before we are on our deathbeds. Would Beatriz ever have come to this conclusion if she had not been given her misdiagnosis? Or would she have continued to put this important dream off?

To avoid making the same mistake as Beatriz, I suggest the practice of *memento mori*. The phrase, translated from Latin, means roughly, "remember that you must die" and urges us to carry this awareness with us as we go about our everyday lives. I can't think of a better way to be intentional about the regrets we may one day face. This turns the concept of regret from negative to positive. It can help us find the anchors necessary to plan our climb. It is the ultimate motivation.

Memento mori is the concept that we must incorporate knowledge of our death into our daily living in order to be more intentional.

Purpose, then, becomes the antidote. All we have to do is take action.

ACTION REGRET

Although we do talk of action regret with the dying, it is usually not as prominent. People on their deathbeds certainly feel bad about actions that hurt relationships, harmed other people, or ruined attempts to accomplish important things. But in reality, these are often inaction regrets in disguise. What we really feel bad about is that we didn't have the courage to fix those hurt relationships, apologize to those we wronged, or try again to accomplish those important things.

Action regret is much more an issue with the living. We recognize that which we have done wrong in the past but feel powerless to go back and right the previous wrongs. Action regret, in this manner, is very past oriented. It is how we cognitively feel about mistakes we have already committed. In other words, it is the purview not only of purpose, but of meaning.

If you remember, happiness is beholden to the concepts of meaning and purpose. Meaning is how we think about and come to terms with the past; while purpose is present and future oriented. The process of dealing with action regrets is first to examine how we feel about this episode in the past. What stories do we tell ourselves about it? Were we victims, knights, or knaves? Resolving these regrets means practicing some of the skills we discussed with narrative therapy. We need to find peace with our past and rewrite the story to separate the idea of *doing* bad things from *being bad* people.

While in therapy, Christine had to do just that. She had to rewrite the past to recognize that she may have been naïve and careless on the day the tragedy happened, but she was not a *bad* person on the inside. She was also a victim. This does not release her from ultimate responsibility, but assigning a different sense of meaning will change everything when it comes to her ability to maneuver in the present and future.

This therapy allowed Christine to give enough importance to the horrible event to move forward and build a life of purpose in the here and now. Her regret about texting and driving turned into a climb to help as many people as she could avoid becoming victims of the same thing. In this scenario, she could empathize not only with the poor child whose life she took, but also with herself.

The good—if any good can come of such a situation—is that Christine used her action regret to build a life of meaning and purpose and to help others. She had a suitable anchor to create a climb. That climb cannot cosmically fix the death of her young victim, but it will ensure that only one life was lost on that horrendous day.

AGENCY: WHY REGRET IS BETTER THAN DISAPPOINTMENT

Although we think of regret in pessimistic terms, there is quite a bit to be optimistic about. As Daniel Pink discusses in his book *The Power of Regret*, the beauty of this emotion is that it grants us agency.[51] When Christine's parents found out that she was texting and driving, they felt a great deal of what they thought was regret but was more accurately disappointment. Ultimately, they couldn't do anything about it. When the dying think about all that they haven't accomplished, maybe we should rename what they are feeling as disappointment. Especially if it is too late for change. They lack agency.

When it comes to regrets, however, *we have agency*. Beatriz could start making jewelry because she wasn't dead yet (and, as it happened, wasn't truly dying). Christine cannot go back and erase the day she made her horrible mistake, but she has the agency to help others not become victims of the same thing. Having agency has the potential to turn regret into purpose. We are one step away from beginning a new climb.

In this scenario, purpose can lead to a sense of diminishing regret. It is the antidote.

If we want to die a good and regret-free death, we have to live a good and regret-free life. The way to do this is *not* to try to avoid regret at all costs. It is simply impossible to do that. Often the only way to recognize regret is in hindsight. Instead, we need to embrace our regrets and realize that they can lead to greater happiness. They do this through meaning and purpose. Meaning involves reassessing the past. Purpose involves using those regrets as anchors to build more climbs.

We need to stop looking at regrets as either negative or positive. Without them, we may never come to terms with that which could have been. Instead, imagine that they are calls to action, yearnings unfulfilled. They are moments in our past when we could have done more and been better. The future then becomes our playground to rewrite these narratives.

If we do attribute any negativity to regret, we must realize that the antidote is in front of us. All we have to do is flip the script. Pursuing little P purpose will remove the associated anxiety and engage us in enjoyable activities that conquer regret by the simple fact of just showing up.

BIG P PURPOSE CREATES DISAPPOINTMENT, NOT REGRET

Pursuing big audacious goals and making them central to your sense of happiness is an exceedingly good way to create a life of disappointment. Given that big P Purpose is often based on an ideal that is hard to achieve, we are likely to be left with not only failure, but a plethora of reasons why we fell short. We either didn't try hard enough or we tried too hard.

We zigged when we should have zagged. We gave up too quickly or not quickly enough.

Failure and disappointment go hand in hand. When we set our goals so high that they are unachievable, we lose the agency to bring about the desired outcome. That's why I consider this disappointment instead of regret. Disappointment is actually worse.

I have experienced this many times in my own life. My years spent becoming a doctor and starting private practice were littered with what I thought was regret but now recognize as disappointment. I used to say that I regretted the day I messed up in front of my attending physician during my internal medicine rotation in my third year of medical school and lost my chance at getting an honors grade. That failure made it unlikely that I would get into a top-ranked residency program or become the academic physician of my dreams—a failure which, in retrospect, I had very little control over. It was just bad luck.

I used to say I regretted the day in the intensive care unit that I wasn't good enough and a patient died. I beat myself up for years about my lack of experience and knowledge. Today, however, I realize that I was placed in a situation for which I didn't have adequate training or experience. I was disappointed with the outcome. I had no agency at the time to have done better. I was a young person with good intentions stuck in a bad situation. I was not, however, a *bad* person. It took me years to come to terms with this.

I used to say I regretted so many moments in the clinic when my schedule wasn't full enough, my skills weren't great enough, or my salary wasn't high enough. Yet I was one of the most successful doctors in my practice or at my hospital. I was disappointed because I was giving it all I could but was still coming up short.

These "regrets" were all based on outsized goals that relied on day-to-day activities that I no longer enjoyed. I felt little agency. In retrospect, I was more disappointed than regretful. The solution was not to accomplish these huge goals, or even to create purpose around activities that didn't fill me up, but instead to build a life of a smaller but more mighty type of purpose. That purpose drove me to pursue activities that felt gratifying just in the process of showing up.

By focusing on little P purpose, I was able to escape the mirage created by being a physician, and see clearly that there were true regrets (not disappointments) that I still had to address. I regretted not spending more time writing and podcasting. I regretted not putting time into writing a book. I regretted that I was unable to create a community because I didn't feel genuine connections to the people I surrounded myself with. These were truly regrets—I had agency to change them. All I had to do was create climbs around my sense of purpose and the regrets melted away.

And that's exactly what I did. Years later, I can honestly say that I rarely feel regret in my life. I have built a number of climbs that address those aspects of my life that I was neglecting. By doing this, I feel a greater sense of peace and less anxiety. I practice *memento mori*.

Would I have any regrets if I died tomorrow?

I can honestly say *no*. Can you do the same? Can you recognize the disappointments in your life and differentiate them from the regrets? If so, can you start to accept the disappointments and act on those regrets today? There is no better time than the present.

This is an essential step in cracking the purpose code.

A PURPOSE PRESCRIPTION: PERFORMING A REGRET AUDIT

- Clear your schedule for an hour on two separate occasions in the next week. If you can, turn off all electronics or silence your phone. Find a quiet place where you will not be disturbed.

- On a blank sheet of paper, add rows numbered one through ten. Leave enough room to write at least a single sentence by each number.

- Take 30 minutes to sit back in a comfortable chair and think about your biggest life regrets. Close your eyes and ponder on the nagging feelings that nip you in the backside when you are most vulnerable. Again, give yourself grace while doing this. This is not the time to assign blame.

- After 30 minutes, open your eyes and return to your sheet of paper. Can you list your top ten regrets? Don't worry about the order. Also, don't be too concerned about being all-inclusive. You may forget a big regret. That is just fine. You can always repeat these steps later.

- After writing all your regrets down, assess each one separately. Ask yourself these questions:

  - Is it a regret or a disappointment? We have agency to act on regrets, not disappointments.

  - Is it an action regret? Did you do something you cannot take back to cause this regret?

- Is it an inaction regret? Have you failed to pursue that which is important to you?

- Mark each entry with an R(egret) or a D(isappointment), and an A(ction) or an I(naction).

- How many of your entries are disappointments and not regrets? You can perhaps discuss with your therapist—or at least reconsider the stories you tell yourself about them.

- For action regrets, are you saddened by the occurrences or the fact that you have not taken new actions to right the wrongs? Could you build a climb around these new actions?

- For inaction regrets, what is stopping you from taking action now? Could this become a purpose anchor for you? Specifically, what are the limiting beliefs that have stopped you from taking action sooner? Can you overcome them?

Remember, *memento mori*—the awareness of the fact that we will die— can be a boon in everyday life. It spurs us to take action and begin transforming regrets into purpose.

CONCLUSION:
BE LIKE ROMAN, NOT
LIKE MICKEY

HOW TO BUILD A BOAT

Like a flash of lightning, Alan had the same exact inclination just twice in his life: once when he was a teenager and again 40 years later. The word "inclination" is a little soft for our purposes. It was more like a compulsion. So he did what any reasonable person would do—he took action.

The result of the first flash of lightning—a sudden urge to get on the water—was a summer project to build a boat. He only had so much time to accomplish this daunting task before heading off to college, so he decided on a canoe. He spent countless hours in the New Jersey sun as his friends got summer jobs and went to parties. Of course, Alan did some of those things too. But his true passion was building the boat. Months later, ready to go to college, he achieved his goal—he had finally finished his masterpiece.

It was a beauty.

Over the next 40 years, Alan often thought back to those summer months spent in the pursuit of something that brought him real joy. He dreamed of the boat and swore that, when the time was right, he would build a better, bigger vessel. Those dreams did not mean that Alan did not live life to its fullest. He found a profession he loved and built a company. He got married, remarried, had kids and eventually grandkids. There was much joy and many pursuits. A coin-collecting hobby became a business. A passion for tennis became a means of staying in shape. A flair for business and a real estate rental portfolio took him to various properties to paint, clean, and fix. It was a full life and Alan was completely engaged in every minute of it. Most of us would consider him a pretty happy human being. His life was full of climbs, large and small.

But that didn't stop the lightning from flashing again.

In his late 50s, and toward the waning portion of his CEO career, he woke up with the calling to build another boat. The kids were mostly off in college or building families of their own. His wife—who wasn't so excited about turning the garage into a workshop—had her own job and other hobbies to pursue.

Alan quietly did some research and bought a kit to build a much bigger boat than the one of his childhood. And he dove in. Nights and weekends. In between board meetings and business trips out of town. When other people were watching television or relaxing, Alan was out in the garage, tinkering around, building another boat. A process that would take a number of years.

Those years were extremely joyful for Alan. He loved learning and working on the minutiae. Every trip to the garage was an adventure. Over the years, others took notice. A child or grandchild would stop by and lend a helping hand. There was the time when the boat had to be flipped, and over 20 people were invited to the house for lunch and a little workout.

Alan eventually hired a local cabinet maker to build some beautiful custom parts of the cabin. On any given day, he would run out and get Gary a large coffee and they would spend hours in the little space measuring, sanding, and installing. They were both wowed by the beauty of the result of their many hours and weekends of work. Then Alan's boat was finally ready for its maiden voyage.

Over years on the water, and many trips transporting family and friends, Alan became very acquainted with the community of boat lovers who docked their boats in the same harbor. People would stop and admire the fine woodwork so unique to his creation. No one ever saw boats made of wood anymore. A journalist even came to interview Alan for the local newspaper.

That boat, made by Alan's own hands, created quite a bit of joy in many people's lives.

Alan is my stepfather. Years later, while celebrating his 80th birthday, family and friends gathered to honor him and tell stories about the years we had shared with him. As children and grandchildren regaled the crowd with anecdotes, many a story was told about that boat and how it became part of our family.

Think about the countless lessons that have been passed on—how his children and grandchildren were able to see persistence, joy, and engagement. Maybe none of us will build a boat, but I can guarantee you that his creativity and dreams have become a part of all of us. We will tell our own grandchildren about the great wooden boat and the man who dared to build it. We will likely model his behavior and embark on our own outrageous and creative climbs.

Alan's actions and legacy will far outlive his cells and organs. What more could he ask for?

LITTLE P PURPOSE IS EVERYWHERE

If you are not seeing little P purpose in your life and the happiness it brings people, then you are not looking hard enough. You are not paying close enough attention to the people around you. My life is so full of those who have been examples of such purpose, I couldn't possibly document them all in this book.

There was Phyllis, my tutor through elementary and middle school, who helped me overcome my learning disability. I can remember bustling into her office during cold Chicago winters and sitting down to a table already adorned with hot chocolate and pretzels. She didn't have to go to such lengths, but she did. She taught me not only how to read, write, and memorize, but how to be taken care of and loved. I cannot begin to express how much this meant to a shy child who felt unworthy. Phyllis was my first role model for being a true healer. I often thought back to her as I decided how I wanted to interact with my own patients. Her sensitivity, patience, and caring were things I tried to bring to those who came to me in need.

The examples of little P purpose only became more prominent as I got older and moved further through the school system. There was my literature teacher in college who I can still see in my mind's eye. His words ring in my ears, though the details have long faded. He impacted my life and pushed me to think differently and more deeply, and to be more curious. His rewards were often intangible and usually went unrecognized. Yet his joy and passion for the teaching of subjects that clearly lit him up have left an indelible mark on thousands of students who passed through his doors. Without such amazing communicators in my life, I probably would have never written my first book. That book has reached tens of thousands of people and can hopefully bring positive change in their lives.

And don't let me forget Bone Marrow Bob and Respiratory Rick, who created colorful examples during my medical school education. Bob was a lab technician who had become the world's expert in teaching students and residents how to perform bone marrow biopsies—a procedure necessary to diagnose cancers and other blood disorders. He was simply the best, and taught students with a zeal and love that were hard to replicate. Rick was a respiratory therapist at the Veterans Administration Hospital during residency. He roamed the halls late at night and helped residents place a breathing tube into spiraling patients who could no longer breathe for themselves. As I became responsible for teaching medical students and residents, I often reflected on the joy that Bob and Rick demonstrated as they taught me.

As I said: if you're not finding these examples in your own life, look harder. The other day my wife was buying a Coach purse on eBay and had questions about its authenticity. Would you believe that there is a guy who is an ex-Coach employee who will authenticate purses with a picture and an identifier code? All you have to do is send him the information. He won't even charge you. Can you believe it? He takes the time to perform these tasks because of his deep belief in the company and his hope to protect others who love the products he spent his career working on.

Little P purpose is everywhere. Just look for the person who is doing something over and over again that provides no or minimal monetary gain. They keep doing these activities because they are important to them.

Wouldn't you like to be engaged in the same? But don't just note these people's presence—interact with them. Find out what fuels their passion and learn to light the same fires in yourself.

By reading this book, you are seeing me engage in my little P purpose. These words are a result of me pursuing a number of climbs that have pushed me to think deeply about the role purpose plays in our lives. Whether it be podcasting or public speaking, the knowledge and insight I have gained have left their mark throughout these pages. This is part of the legacy that I want to leave to you. My hope is for these words to live on long after I am gone.

CRACKING THE CODE

I wrote this book to help you figure out how to crack the purpose code—to help you overcome the paradoxical nature of this important entity and grab all the good and leave all the bad behind. In order to do this, Part 1 focused on the magic of little P purpose. Purpose has never been and shouldn't be a four-letter word. Although studies find that purpose anxiety is not only real but pervasive, that doesn't mean we should avoid the question of purpose altogether. Purpose in life is associated with us living longer, healthier, and happier lives.

But how to unlock it?

There are two types of purpose, with two very different characteristics. Little P purpose is the kind that is focused on process and less on product. It is goal-agnostic although not goal-phobic. This small type of purpose focuses on abundance. All you have to do is show up.

Big P Purpose, on the other hand, is goal oriented and traps us in a scarcity mindset. While goals seem great at the start, when it comes to purpose, we really don't want to focus on activities that we can fail. Furthermore, even success leads to either the push to achieve more or the fear of losing what we have gained. Either way, we lose.

Just understanding the difference between the types of purpose, however, is not enough. For many, anxiety surrounds how we go about *finding* our sense of purpose. The mistake here is to think that it is something we find. Purpose is actually something we create. To do this, we concentrate on realizing which activities or joys we can anchor our purpose in. It turns out that there are several techniques. And if none of those work, we can throw a bunch of spaghetti against the wall and see what sticks.

Embracing this concept of purpose, we see that while money does much for us, it is just a tool. This tool is one powerful way to create time and space to better assess what purpose should really look like in our life. You don't need money to pursue the important things in life, and having a lot of money will not ensure that you are happy. You can't earn the type of life you want to live; you have to create it.

In Part 2 of this book, we used this understanding to build a concept of happiness. Happiness, it turns out, has two components. Meaning is our cognitive understanding of the past. Building happiness is the process of rewriting the stories of past trauma and separating ourselves from the bad things that happened. In doing so, we become the heroes of our own story. While meaning is all about the past, it is the reimagining of this past that is essential to creating a good present and future.

Purpose, on the other hand, is all about the present and future. These are the activities in the here and now that create a sense of community and connections. In Chapter 6, I shared a framework for little P purpose called the climb. The climb is happiness in action. It is the way we incorporate meaning and then build a life of those activities that fulfill us. Those activities, of course, are all about little P purpose.

But what if you can't afford climbing shoes? We come up with all sorts of excuses to delay our climbs. Whether material resources or scarcity of time, there is always a reason not to take the first steps up the mountain. Most climbs actually cost almost no money. When we realize that material wealth is but one tool in an overflowing toolbelt, we have greater agency in getting past our own limiting beliefs about what we can and can't accomplish.

And finally, in Part 3, we discussed why it all matters. Although people can never be our purpose, the whole point of purpose is to create connections, community, and eventually a legacy. We do this with and for other people. This is what winning looks like. We build these intentional communities of people around us in the process of pursuing little P purpose. Instead of passing on generational trauma, we create generational growth.

That growth affects those we interact with, both our contemporaries as well as our descendants. This is our true and lasting legacy.

Then, and only then, will we truly minimize regrets. As discussed in the last chapter, regrets are actions or inactions which we had some agency to do differently or better. By creating climbs of purposeful activities around these regrets, we in essence are administering our own antidote. We should not confuse regret with disappointment. Disappointments surround big audacious goals for which we simply didn't have the skills or luck to succeed.

POSTSCRIPT

Roman lost his battle with cancer over 30 years ago. He had a rare form of malignancy that proved resistant to treatment. I had spent a little less than five years with him. Yet his effect on me was profound. Thirty years later, I am still talking about him and what his little store meant to me.

I am not the only one. There were ten or 15 of us kids who frequented the shop. Like me, many were misfits and outcasts who, up to that point, had been struggling to find a sense of community and belonging. Century's did that for us. Many left Roman's tutelage to go on to bigger and more complete lives. Some—like me—became doctors. No doubt others became accountants, and rocket scientists, and lawyers. We left those doors with a new sense of confidence that would affect just about every other aspect of our lives.

And those ripples in the ocean caused by one man's actions continue to ebb and flow. Those kids grew up to make their mark on the world. How many lives can a doctor's actions affect? How much money can an accountant save their clients? How much justice can a lawyer help their clients achieve? Each of these moments was set in motion years ago by a man who has already passed away.

Many of us have had children. And somewhere in some dime store, a father is buying his daughter her first pack of baseball cards and they might just be splitting that godawful piece of bubblegum (if they even still come in each wax pack). Roman's legacy remains. He has had a major impact on me, as well as countless others in this world. His legacy has become exponential.

But you know who has had almost no impact on my life? Mickey Mantle. That's right: Mickey Mantle, whose baseball cards I so zealously hunted for during childhood. Mickey Mantle, who broke countless records and undoubtedly was one of the premier players to have ever played the sport of baseball. I rarely think of Mickey Mantle; and even if I did, he has had no positive effect on my life.

Now, I can hear you argue the opposite. Mickey may have not affected my life, but there undoubtedly were others who took Mickey's example and set off to become baseball players themselves or break their own records. While I cannot argue the truth of that, I do know for a fact that if Mickey Mantle was your source of big audacious purpose, then most likely you failed.

For every million kids out there who worshipped Mickey Mantle, or Babe Ruth, or Willie Mays, there is probably only one who made it to major league baseball. Which means, of course, that 999,999 failed. That is almost 1 million people walking around with purpose anxiety today, feeling a profound sense of disappointment.

Not one of the professional baseball players whose cards I collected meant as much to me as Roman. Not one of them will have such a great impact.

In closing, I wish for you to have a life of little P purpose. I wish for you to use that purpose to build communities of people you love and who love you. I hope that they become your teachers and students, mentors and friends. I wish for you to impact so many people that, like the pebble dropped in the ocean, your legacy will last decades and centuries after you have left this world.

I wish for you to be like Roman and not Mickey.

GLOSSARY

The **achievement treadmill** refers to the concept that people tend to return to a relative stable baseline of happiness regardless of goal achievement.

Action regret focuses on the wish to have acted in a different way at a key moment or the wish that we could go back and do better.

The **art of subtraction** is the process of removing things from your life that no longer serve you.

Big P Purpose is a goal-oriented purpose that is often outsized and easy to fail at. It is often associated with anxiety.

Burnout is work-related stress associated with physical and emotional exhaustion and loss of identity.

Communities of internal purpose exist to take care of themselves and are made up of individuals who come together to support each other, learn, and grow.

A *deus ex machina* is a literary device or last-minute plot twist that resolves a storyline.

The **Easterlin Paradox** is the theory that at any given point, happiness and income are directly correlated but over the long term they are no longer related.

Emotional wellbeing is how a person feels on a daily basis.

Financial independence is the state of having saved and invested enough money to not need to work ever again.

The **free-time paradox** describes how the wealthier have less leisure time than the less wealthy.

Flow describes being totally engaged or engrossed in an activity.

Generational growth is the opposite of generational trauma. These are the positive scripts passed down from our ancestors.

Generational trauma is the transferring of traumatic experiences or stressors from one generation to the next.

Geoarbitrage is the process of making money in a high cost of living area and then moving to a low cost of living area.

To be **goal agnostic** is to be unaffected or not concerned with goals.

Hedonic adaption refers to the notion that after positive events and a subsequent increase in positive feelings, people return to a relatively stable baseline.

Human capital refers to the skills, knowledge, and experience possessed by an individual or population.

Impostor syndrome is the inability to believe that one's success is deserved.

Inaction regrets are regrets of omission, commonly encountered among the dying.

Incremental gain is the process of improving in small sequential steps.

Keeping up with the Joneses is a phrase that describes doing something in order to show that you have as much money as other people.

Your **legacy** is the things you do today that will last long after you die in the people who knew and loved you.

Life evaluation is a person's long-term sense of accomplishment or satisfaction.

Limiting beliefs are mistaken beliefs about yourself that limit you in some way.

Little P purpose is process-oriented purpose that is impossible to fail. It is often associated with health, longevity, and happiness.

Loss Aversion is the overwhelming fear of losing something we have worked very hard to gain.

Margin is the amount by which a thing either is won or falls short. In the case of winning, it is the little bit extra.

Meaning is a process focused on cognition and our ability to connect ideas and make sense of our past.

Memento mori is the concept that we must incorporate knowledge of our death into our daily living in order to be more intentional.

Money scripts are your unconscious beliefs about money, often rooted in childhood, that affect your adult behaviors and perspectives.

The **myth of joyful parenthood** is a myth of parental joy that parents have collectively created because otherwise we would have a hard time justifying the huge investment that kids require.

A **poorhouse** is a place maintained at public expense to house needy or dependent persons.

Purpose anchors are themes around which we can start to create our climbs. These themes are based on little P purpose.

Purpose anxiety is the fear of not knowing your purpose in life.

Purpose in life is the term researchers use to measure the extent to which a respondent perceives a general sense of meaning and purpose in life.

Quiet quitting is putting minimal effort in to keep a job but refusing to go the extra mile.

Regret is the feeling of sadness or remorse over a past action, decision, or choice.

Rugged individualism is the belief that all individuals can succeed without help from outside sources or the government.

A **side hustle** is an extra job or hobby that one does in addition to their regular job that produces extra revenue.

The climb is a framework for building a life of little P purpose.

Time scarcity is the feeling that there is not enough time to do important things.

A **vicious cycle** is the opposite of a virtuous cycle. It is a self-perpetuating sequence of events with an ever-increasing negative outcome.

ENDNOTES

1   https://thesimplyluxuriouslife.com/juliachildlacouronne/.

2   https://medium.com/@robroy_63706/how-did-julia-childs-true-purpose-establish-a-6-million-dollar-legacy-a3a3795a7384.

3   https://jamanetwork.com/journals/jamanetworkopen/fullarticle/2734064.

4   https://www.ncbi.nlm.nih.gov/pmc/articles/PMC7494628/.

5   https://www.researchgate.net/publication/232566815_Purpose_in_life_What_is_its_relationship_to_happiness_depression_and_grieving.

6   https://link.springer.com/article/10.1007/s10902-023-00625-7.

7   https://www.forbes.com/sites/tracybrower/2023/03/13/managers-play-a-crucial-role-leaders-react-to-employee-mental-health/?sh=10710d504333.

8   https://www.researchgate.net/publication/304087988_The_Search_for_Purpose_in_Life_An_Exploration_of_Purpose_the_Search_Process_and_Purpose_Anxiety.

9   https://ourworldindata.org/life-expectancy.

10 https://www.cdc.gov/pcd/issues/2019/19_0017.htm.

11 https://www.fool.com/research/average-retirement-age/#:~:text=The%20average%20retirement%20age%20has,to%2021.3%20years%20for%20women.

12 https://www.npr.org/2023/05/16/1176206568/less-important-religion-in-lives-of-americans-shrinking-report#:~:text=In%202019%2C%2019%25%20of%20Americans,a%20few%20times%20a%20year.%22

13 https://www.latimes.com/archives/la-xpm-2000-jan-20-mn-55828-story.html.

14   https://www.theguardian.com/film/2018/mar/08/hedy-lamarr-1940s-bombshell-helped-invent-wifi-missile#:~:text=Although%20she%20achieved%20international%20fame,practised%20her%20favourite%20hobby%3A%20inventing.

15   https://www.womenshistory.org/education-resources/biographies/hedy-lamarr#:~:text=Hedy%20Lamarr%20was%20an%20Austrian,GPS%2C%20and%20Bluetooth%20communication%20systems.

16   https://attractionsmagazine.com/walt-disney-most-inspiring-quote-isnt-actually-his/.

17   https://www.zippia.com/advice/how-many-people-lie-on-resumes-survey/.

18   https://www.nytimes.com/2015/07/02/world/europe/nicholas-winton-is-dead-at-106-saved-children-from-the-holocaust.html.

19   https://pubmed.ncbi.nlm.nih.gov/14017386/.

20   https://www.frontiersin.org/articles/10.3389/fpsyt.2023.1077665/full.

21   https://pubmed.ncbi.nlm.nih.gov/22788983/.

22   https://continuagroup.com/article/lifetime-legacies-life-review-questions/#:~:text=What%20challenges%20and%20joys%20did,any%20regrets%20or%20unfulfilled%20dreams%3F.

23   https://www.pnas.org/doi/full/10.1073/pnas.1011492107.

24   Proc. Natl. Acad. Sci. U.S.A. 118, e2016976118 (2021).

25   https://www.pnas.org/doi/10.1073/pnas.2208661120#executive-summary-abstract.

26   https://www.sciencedaily.com/releases/2021/02/210208161922.htm.

27   https://www.iza.org/publications/dp/13923/the-easterlin-paradox#:~:text=The%20Easterlin%20Paradox%20states%20that,the%20contradiction%20is%20social%20comparison.

28   https://psycnet.apa.org/buy/2022-50413-001.

29   https://www.researchgate.net/publication/22451114_Lottery_Winners_and_Accident_Victims_Is_Happiness_Relative.

30   https://www.sofi.su.se/english/2.17851/research/research-news/a-large-lottery-win-makes-us-more-content-with-life-but-not-necessarily-happier-1.512911.

31   https://news.harvard.edu/gazette/story/2017/04/over-nearly-80-years-harvard-study-has-been-showing-how-to-live-a-healthy-and-happy-life/.

32   https://en.wikipedia.org/wiki/Hero%27s_journey.

33   https://pubmed.ncbi.nlm.nih.gov/25968138/.

34   https://www.researchgate.net/publication/343921003_Everything_is_Story_
Telling_Stories_and_Positive_Psychology.

35   https://www.apa.org/monitor/2011/01/stories#:~:text=And%2C%20in%20
a%20yet%2Dunpublished,it%20'til%20you%20make%20it.

36   https://www.verywellmind.com/how-storytelling-is-good-for-your-
mental-health-5199744

37   https://www.scholars.northwestern.edu/en/publications/telling-better-
stories-competence-building-narrative-themes-incre

38   https://www.psychologytoday.com/us/therapy-types/narrative-therapy.

39   https://www.researchgate.net/publication/334822458_Engaging_in_
Personally_Meaningful_Activities_is_Associated_with_Meaning_Salience_
and_Psychological_Well-being.

40   https://www.tandfonline.com/doi/full/10.1080/01490400.2022.2056550.

41   https://www.ncbi.nlm.nih.gov/pmc/articles/PMC8448794/.

42   https://www.theatlantic.com/business/archive/2016/09/the-free-time-
paradox-in-america/499826/.

43   https://www.cdc.gov/pcd/issues/2019/19_0017.htm.

44   https://psychcentral.com/health/genetic-trauma#how-can-trauma-
be-passed-down.

45   https://www.psychologicalscience.org/news/were-only-human/the-
myth-of-joyful-parenthood.html#:~:text=They%20suspect%20that%20the%20
belief,huge%20investment%20that%20kids%20require.

46   https://medium.com/together-institute/why-do-communities-exist-for-
internal-or-external-purpose-or-both-509a776538c0.

47   https://www.ncbi.nlm.nih.gov/pmc/articles/PMC7585135/.

48   https://www.ncbi.nlm.nih.gov/pmc/articles/PMC2910600/.

49   https://www.science.org/doi/10.1126/science.343.6169.361.

50   https://www.apa.org/monitor/2019/02/legacy-trauma.

51   https://www.atlassian.com/blog/productivity/daniel-pink-regret-
interview#:~:text=Career%2D%20and%20education%2Drelated%20
regrets,forces%20behind%20the%20Great%20Resignation.